For all the problem horses

Contents

Evidence indicates that the horse was domesticated at around the end of the 2nd millennium BC. Since that time, the horse has been used as a vehicle of war, a form of transport, a draft animal in agriculture and, more recently, for leisure and sporting pursuits. Our knowledge of horse training was passed down to us from our ancestors. Sometimes these methods include mythologies that are not only difficult for the horse to fathom but also can result in poor welfare. For example, the flight response is commonly incorporated in training, yet it has a disastrous legacy, with problems that are likely to come back to haunt the rider or handler in later years.

Enlightened school teachers these days do their best not to use fear as a tool or weapon in a child's learning process. The same should be applied to animals undergoing training because the same problems arise with them when fear-inducing techniques are used. Fear associations are indelible and problems include the creation of negative associations with people and the disinclination to try new responses in new learning situations. It is small wonder that the domestic horse accounts for more human deaths and injuries than any other domestic animal, and that research shows that around two-thirds of horses that are sent to slaughter are sent for behavioral reasons.

We owe it to the horse to do a better job of training, especially since we use him not for survival but for our own leisure, ego, and glory. This amounts to a reorganization of the way we do things to horses in training. One of Ryan Gingerich's great attributes that I first noticed on meeting him and working with him is his open-mindedness. He was prepared to let go of techniques and ideologies if there was sufficient evidence the other way. That is a rare quality in a person and an even rarer one in the horse world. It is one that I greatly admire. When I first met Ryan, I showed him the system I have developed for dressage horses based on the inherent principles of learning theory, and when I left the United States in 2005, I suggested that Ryan develop a system for Western trainers based also on learning theory. The result is the evolution of Ryan's Connective Horsemanship and finally the birth of this informative book based on a correct interpretation of behavioral science not only in practice but in theoretical explanations, as well.

What is very pleasing is that this book presents a thorough systematic approach—when riders and handlers have achieved certain benchmarks, or when they have problems, they can take the book and read the relevant section, and then go back to train or retrain the horse. I am pleased to be able to recommend *Beyond a Whisper: Training Horses with a New Language from The Behaviorist*. I feel sure that the welfare of the horse is more safeguarded than ever.

Andrew McLean, Dip Ed, BSc, PhD
Australian Equine Behaviour Centre (www.aebc.com.au)
Author of *The Truth About Horses; Academic Horse Training;* and
    Equitation Science (with Paul McGreevy, BVSc, PhD, MRCVS, MACVS)

I believe the principal goal of horse training is to have a controllable and predictable horse. I also believe that meeting this goal is possible for *all* horses if their training is done in a way that capitalizes on their inherent strengths. Training methods that are sequential, consistent, and systematic allow the horse to *learn* rather than simply react. These methods, firmly grounded in the science of animal behaviorism, are the foundation of my program: Connective Horsemanship.

Sadly, the methods of training horses are thought to differ from one discipline to the next. Some riders still claim to rely on the traditional methods of the "Old West." Others say they place their faith on the well-trodden cavalry-based traditions of Europe. Often, enthusiasts believe that their chosen discipline requires a specialized training approach. They may even be unwilling to consider the training methods of someone from a different discipline. This is unfortunate because—ultimately—all trainers desire the same thing: a responsive, willing horse that is a joy to ride.

While Western and English riding may seem entirely different at first glance, they both hold inherently similar principles. They both build upon the same five essential qualities:

- Basic control
- Lightness
- Rhythm
- Line
- Connection to the rider

Regardless of discipline, mastering these five elements first introduced to me by my mentor Dr. Andrew McLean, ensures the horse's responsiveness to the rider's cues. These qualities make the horse more capable and competitive within any equestrian pursuit or discipline. (I discuss Dr. McLean and these elements in more detail on p. 72.)

Connective Horsemanship is dedicated to helping riders incorporate these elements into their training. Trainers who use Connective Horsemanship techniques often discover that their horses learn faster. An added benefit is that behavioral problems are generally eliminated before they become ingrained habits.

Connective Horsemanship is a unique training process and the result of over a decade of research and development. Its mission is to understand and communicate with young, misunderstood, and behaviorally challenged horses. It underscores the importance of the cueing language between the horse and rider, for it is through this "connective language" that understanding builds and communication exists.

This training process emphasizes the importance of the "Go" and "Stop" commands. I believe that *all* behavioral problems stem from a lack of responsiveness to one or both of these commands.

The cueing language we utilize to train our horses must be clear, concise, and consistent. When we fail to follow these simple guidelines, the horse instinctively falls back to his root drive: *fear*. The untrained or poorly handled horse embodies fear. His survival instinct is the strongest and most readily available emotion he possesses. All behavioral issues are tied to this fear response. Developing and refining a clear cueing language makes it possible for trainers to rehabilitate the fear-based behavioral problems in the horses we encounter.

I have been fortunate to work with many horses that have broadened my experiences, furthered my education, and shaped my theories. They have taught me the value of patience, kindness, and honesty. Ultimately, however, they have justified my training philosophies.

I am a horse trainer, a behaviorist, a coach, a friend, a husband, and a father. Like you, I continue to search for ways to bridge the communication gaps between our horses and ourselves. Of course no one has all the answers. But with patience and perseverance, I believe that any trainer can develop a language that allows human and horse to understand each other with far greater clarity than ever before.

Wishing you a lifetime of connective training joys,

Ryan Gingerich, The Behaviorist

Basic Control   The material covered in the first stages of a horse's education, including go, stop, turn left and right, stand still, and back up.

Behaviorism   The psychological school of thought that posits that all learning occurs through objective interaction with the environment.

Cavalry Stop   See "pulley rein."

Conflict Behavior   "Bad behavior" that manifests in horses as bucking, rearing, cribbing, kicking, or biting, to name just a few. All the "problem" behaviors a horse exhibits.

Connective Horsemanship®   An equine training system based upon the school of behaviorism.

Conditioning   The process by which an animal learns to respond to a set of rules or stimuli. During the conditioning process, the animal is repeatedly encouraged to do a particular action in a certain manner.

Continuous Reinforcement   Desired behavior is recognized and rewarded every time it occurs. The reward for the behavior happens without fail on a continuing basis.

Counter Conditioning   See **Deletion.**

Deletion   The process of overlaying an undesirable or inappropriate behavior with a different, desired, conditioned response to the same stimuli. (Also known as "extinction," "counter conditioning," and "over training.")

Differential Reinforcement   Utilizing a combination of both positive and negative reinforcers.

Error-Free Training   A comprehensive training process that does not allow the horse to practice undesirable behaviors and that overlays previously learned unwanted responses with newer, correct actions.

Extinction   See **Deletion.**

Extinction Schedule   A systematic process of deletion.

Fear Response   A physical reaction to something that is perceived as frightening or as a threat.

Fixed Interval Reinforcement   A reinforcer or reward that occurs predictably, at a specific time, without fail. The reward doesn't happen every time the behavior is exhibited, but it happens on a predictable schedule.

Flexion   The lateral turning of the horse's head to the right or the left; a side-to-side movement based at the poll.

Flight Response   The horse's highly developed instinctive desire to run away from anything that frightens him.

Flooding   Rapidly and repeatedly exposing a horse to a stimulus in such a way that the flight response is overloaded or negated in order to rapidly force the horse into exhibiting a new behavior. Flooding works by exhausting the horse either physically or mentally (or both) into submission.

Habituation   The state that occurs (whether desired or not) when a behavior is repeated to the extent that it becomes ingrained and occurs without deliberate effort.

Lightness   The stage of training after a horse has mastered Basic Control. Includes developing relaxation, flexion, and strength.

Line   Direction. When a horse masters "Line," he remains on whatever path the rider chooses while readily responding to basic controls, moving forward with Lightness, and remaining in Rhythm.

Natural Behavior Pattern   Ingrained, instinctive, predictably occurring actions that all members of a species, group, or society exhibit.

Negative Reinforcement   Subtracting or removing something that the subject finds irritating in order to eliminate undesired behavior. The subject associates the correct behavior with the accompanying negative reinforcement and alters his or her actions accordingly.

Operant Conditioning   Conditioned responses based upon the concepts of positive and negative reinforcement. (Also known as "response stimulus" or "RS" conditioning because it forms an association between the animal's response [its behavior] and the stimulus that follows [the consequence of that behavior].)

Over Training   See **Deletion**.

Positive Reinforcement   Adding something that the subject wants whenever it evidences the desired behavior. The subject is likely to more readily repeat the desired behavior in the future, in the hopes of receiving further rewards.

Pulley Rein   An "emergency stop" involving picking up one rein and raising the hand, holding it up high above the horse's ears while moving the hand on the other rein back toward the rider's hips. This is applied quickly, firmly, and decisively. When the pulley rein is applied, the horse's head comes up and his stride becomes short and choppy, generally shortening to the point where he stops. (Also known as a "cavalry stop.")

Reinforcer   Anything that increases a behavior or makes it happen more frequently.

Relaxation   Occurs when the horse is readily compliant to your cues.

Response Stimulus Conditioning / "RS Conditioning"   See **Operant Conditioning**.

Rhythm   The phase of training that addresses the elements of timing, balance, impulsion, and speed control; all of which are necessary for the horse to master before progressing to higher levels of training.

Shaping See **Successive Approximation**.

Social Behaviors Actions that happen within a group of individuals of the same species that affect the group's society as a whole.

Successive Approximation Methodically changing an animal's behavior over time through step-by-step, sequential training that incrementally leads toward a desired, targeted response. (Also called "shaping.")

Systematic Desensitization Gradually introducing the horse to something he fears by introducing the object of fear so slowly, and in such a deliberate, non-aggressive way that the horse never feels compelled to access his flight response.

Variable Interval Reinforcement A reinforcer or reward is distributed at random times (but only after the desired behavior is exhibited).

PART ONE

Developing a New Language for Horse and Human

An Essential **History of the Horse**

To understand the horse's history is to understand the horse. By 4,000 years ago, according to archaeological evidence, the horse was found throughout what is now modern Europe, from the British Isles to Western Asia.

The horse is a relative newcomer when it comes to having a relationship with man. In fact, the horse is only one of a dozen species of mammals that has survived domestication. The ancient Egyptians attempted to domesticate many different animals, such as hyenas, ibex, antelopes, and gazelles. The Native Americans kept pet raccoons, bears, and even moose. Yet none of these remain domesticated today.

Why?

It's a matter of acceptance. The horse is a social being. He needs others to survive and thrive. When he cannot socialize and interact with his own kind, the horse begins to socially adapt and form bonds with other creatures in order to fulfill this need for acceptance. These social bonds are what made it possible for the horse to become accustomed to a wide variety of physical settings and environmental situations.

Because of both the Ice Age and man's encroachment on the grassy steppes of Europe, the environment of the horse changed. The plains were less fertile. The grass held less sustenance for horses. They were forced to rely on man for food, water, and—at some point—companionship.

The first people to domesticate the horse weren't neophytes when it came to handling livestock. They had been raising goats and cows for many thousands of years before the domestication of the horse. Their understanding of animal husbandry allowed them to successfully breed, care for, and utilize the horse in a way that was mutually beneficial to both horses and humans.

Domestication doesn't mean that humans immediately began riding or driving these beasts of burden. It only means that they utilized horses in a manner that helped the people lead a better life.

Compelling archaeological evidence indicates that man first used the horse as a food resource before using it as a means of transportation. There came a time in our mutual history, however, when a human discovered the value of keeping the livestock "live."

1.1   *The history of humans and horses is a long one. Cave paintings of horses at Lascaux, in southwestern France, are an estimated 16,000 years old.*

According to Dr. David W. Anthony, an archeologist at Hartwick College in Oneonta, New York, the first known horsemen may have occurred as early as 4,000 BC. They came from the Sredni Stog culture that lived on the grasslands along the Dnieper River in what is now the Ukraine. Thousands of bones have been found piled up in archaeological sites of the Sredni Stog, notably the site of Dereivka. Some archaeologists estimate that 50 percent of all the inhabitants' meat came from horses. However, some of the teeth in the horses' remains bear distinctive bit-marks. Since the wheel had not yet been invented at the time (and would not be invented until nearly 1,000 years later), the obvious conclusion is that the bit was in the horse's mouth because someone was on the horse's back.

Imagine what possessed that first crazy person who decided to climb on the back of a horse. It must have been a wild ride!

In Dr. Andrew McLean's book, *The Truth About Horses*, he uses the following analogy to illustrate the process of the horse coming to humans:

> *What might have happened if a fleet of aircraft had appeared on earth thousands of years ago? The local inhabitants, once they had overcome their fear, would have fallen victim to their own curiosity. After much experimentation, and many failed attempts, someone—somehow—would have made one of the planes fly.*

I believe this is a true and accurate depiction of the first ride. The horse was like those big, shiny planes. They were as foreign to the people

1.2   *The horse gave the human race a way to flourish. Horses allowed man to go further, faster. They made it possible for tribes to establish trade with other, far-off cultures. Horses also allowed for swift and devastating attacks on neighboring cultures. They enabled some tribes to conquer others. They helped stronger civilizations to survive and spread. Small wonder that the horse was revered and highly valued.*

of the steppes of Europe as an alien craft would be to us. However, like Dr. McLean proposes, eventually, we would get over our fears. Curiosity would take over. We would attempt to make one of these alien crafts fly, and wouldn't give up until we had mastered the skill.

In any case, at some point, perhaps due to deforestation and the need for larger territories, or possibly for a desire for military advantage, someone somehow learned to take control of the beasts and rode them to ultimate success.

To know the horse is to know ourselves. The horse literally made humanity what it is today. He is an integral part of our very existence.

A Common Language

Any discussion on the role scientific principles play in improving our interaction with horses is fraught with difficulty. Some people consider "science" as an unpleasant high school memory involving dissection and tiny, uncooperative frogs. Others take issue with applying a field that is often perceived as cold and reserved to a creature as beautiful and sensitive as the horse.

At its heart, however, all training that involves a proven system and that successfully shapes animal behavior is based upon science.

When I say *science*, I am talking about an effort to increase human understanding of how the physical world works through controlled methods. Scientists collect data on observable, physical evidence of natural phenomena and analyze this information to explain what and how things work.

Animal behavior is a field of study dedicated to understanding how the animal world works. There are two major parts to animal behavior. There is the study of *ethology*, a rapidly growing field of zoology dedicated to studying the patterns of how animals behave in their natural habitat. And there is also *psychology*, the study of how the human mental processes influence behavior. Today, many research areas encompass animal behavior, like neuropsychology, applied ethology, and evolutionary psychology.

When science is the center of your training philosophy, some things must be excluded. Leave out any kind of tendency toward anthropomorphism. Disregard feelings, hunches, and things of that nature. Horses are *not* humans. Ascribing human motivations and emotions to horses only serves to widen the communication gap between species, instead of bridging it.

2.1 *The flight response—the reason horses shy and spook—is hardwired into every equine brain. It is why horses have survived. Without it, there would be no horses today.*

Just Watch

Every interaction we have with the horse affects the horse in some way, because we are always affecting or changing the horse's behavior, depending upon *our* behavior. If, however, we take a hands-off approach and simply observe, we can gain greater understanding of how the horse interprets the world. No matter the situation, we can learn something every day if we take the time to watch how the horse interacts with other horses and other people.

In fact, this approach is exactly what I do when I do "an evaluation" of someone's horse. It is the critical first step in my training process. I watch. I just observe the horse in his natural state, and when interacting with people, and see what insights I can glean from doing that. I then take those observations and examine them through the lens of my experience with horses. Generally, this process allows me to say with confidence why the horse is reacting the way he is.

You don't have to observe long to realize that horses live for three things: *food, comfort,* and *safety.*

➥   If left alone, horses are content to graze for the better part of the day.

➥   Horses obtain comfort primarily through social interactions with other horses.

➥   Since horses are prey animals, they want to stay in a group because there is safety in numbers.

The need for safety has resulted in a highly developed *flight response*—the desire to flee first and ask questions later. The horse's flight response colors every aspect of my training method, Connective Horsemanship®. The entire program is about understanding the horse's innate desire to run away, and helping the horse to understand that flight is not necessary. (I discuss my method in detail beginning on pg. 67.)

Let's Come to an Understanding

An understanding of science helps to define how horses work, how they learn, how they interact with each other, and how they relate to you and me. Understanding *that* gives way to better husbandry practices and better training processes. It's all part of how a better understanding of science on our part has a direct impact on the horse's quality of life.

The way humans think is not exactly the way horses think. Understanding how horses learn, how horses react, how horses think, and how memories are produced in their mind gives us a better opportunity to connect with them because we are more able to communicate with them on their own level. It frees us from always trying to place our own beliefs and our own thought processes on them.

LIVE AND LEARN

Because of the way the equine brain is wired, the horse continues to learn all his life. To the horse, however, learning is associated more with *memory* than with *deduction* or *intuition*. In a nutshell, the horse learns through consistent, repetitive cues or stimuli from the outside world.

The horse's brain functions in such a way that it can remember vast quantities of experiences. The horse's mid-brain—the "memory bank"—contains the largest and most developed portions of his brain. The equine central nervous system spends a considerable amount of energy keeping the memory bank protected and working.

The horse's memory informs equine learning behavior. It allows horses to learn very quickly, which keeps them from getting hurt. If, for instance, a horse doesn't learn to back off when another horse flicks his tail, or raises a hind foot, or twitches his ears back, or tightens up his mouth, or rolls his eyes in a certain way, the potential for injury is great. If a horse doesn't learn to recognize potential threats and immediately react to them, he puts not only himself, but also the entire herd at risk. Without memory-based learning behavior, the horse would never have survived.

THE EMOTIONAL HORSE

Do horses have emotions? I am often asked this question, and for years, my answer had always been "No." Horses are simple animals that are unable to reason and have no conscious perception of self. Such a simple creature surely cannot process the complex information that is involved with emotions. In recent years, however, my research into the equine mind opened my eyes to a possibility that my assumptions may have been incorrect. This led me to ask another question: If horses *do* possess the ability to have emotions, then how does this impact the way we train, house, and interact with them?

My quest for answers led me to Dr. Temple Grandin's exploration of the subject. Dr. Grandin—author of the best-selling *Animals in Translation* and *Animals Make Us Human*—makes a strong case for animals having emotions. She describes emotions as either *simple* or *complex*. Simple emotions are fear, rage, discovery, confusion, gain, loss, happiness and depression. Complex emotions are shame, guilt, embarrassment, greed, respect, and contempt.

Dr. Grandin suggests that the ability to experience simple emotions is not limited to humans. She also notes that animals are unable to have mixed emotions, that they are not ambivalent about anything, and that they don't have love-hate relationships. As humans these emotions are second nature to us. We don't think about being unable to express joy or sorrow, empathy or indifference.

The differences between horse and human are much more than meta-physical. The horse lacks the complexity that makes up the human brain.

Emotions come from the cerebral cortex and in humans this area of the brain is very well developed. Research has shown us that the measure of intelligence is based on the number of folds in the brain and brain size to body ratio of the organism. Horses have relatively small brains with little folding. The more folds in a brain, the greater the overall size; thus the greater the animal's intelligence. This does not mean that horses are not intelligent. (In fact, many studies show the horse as having a highly developed memory, as I mentioned before. A horse can recall past experiences and react to them readily.) It merely shows the horse's intelligence in relation to humans.

After months of reading and studying and observing my horses, I now believe that horses do feel the simple emotions of fear, anger, confusion, and possibly happiness. I can say for sure that a horse doesn't feel these emotions like you and I. The way emotions are processed in the human brain is different from the horse because of the compartmentalization of the horse's brain. We as humans have the ability to reason through why we feel a particular way. Horses simply feel emotion but don't have the ability to rationalize their reasons for feeling.

This knowledge should inform the way we train our horses. First, we must realize that horses cannot feel animosity or contempt toward us. Their misbehaviors aren't premeditated attempts at "getting back at us." They are simply expressions of what the horse is feeling at that given time. If the horse feels fearful, he reacts out of fear. If the horse is unsure and confused about a situation, uncertainty governs his reactions. You wouldn't punish a child because he was scared or confused. Nor would you use fear and intimidation to try to teach a child a new word or life lesson. You wouldn't do this to your children and you shouldn't punish a horse for his feelings, either. My goal as a clinician is to get across to the general horse public that horses can become confused when confronted with opposing cues, or similar cues that are too close together.

Your horse is a living, feeling creature that—when pressed into a stressful environment—will do what he thinks is best for himself, not what is best for you. That may mean the horse bucks you off, runs away with you, or generally misbehaves. These misbehaviors are what the horse thinks he needs and what he feels will make the pressures oppressing him go away.

It is your responsibility to accept the possibility that you may be causing many of the misbehaviors your horse is expressing. Horses are products of their environment. Bad training yields bad results. Inconsistent training yields inconsistent results.

As I think back to time spent with my mentor Dr. Andrew McLean, I am reminded of a conversation we once had about the emotional horse. His view was always that horses have limited emotions. He said, "Equine emotions are not a result of prefrontal cortical input (like ours), and they have a less dopamine-driven frontal lobe so their emotions don't go into deep depressions or euphoric highs (like ours)."

If we don't understand what the horse is feeling, then we as feeling beings find it hard to relate. We become confused when our training goes wrong, which translates to our horses. We are quick to blame the horse for his mistakes and never fully realize that the problem is truly our fault. We are the teachers, and our horses are our students. Our lessons should always be clearer to *us* than to *them*.

So how does one become better at communicating with the horse? The key is knowledge. We must never stop learning and developing new and better ways of explaining what we want and understanding the horse's response. Do horses possess the ability to feel simple emotions? Yes they do. Do they feel and process these emotions the way humans do? No. This simple knowledge should change the way we interact with our horses and how we train them. It should make us realize that horses can feel pain, fear, loneliness, confusion, sadness, and possibly happiness. It means that every time we scare our horse with improper training techniques and use improper training equipment, we cause irreparable damage to him and move a step further from our ultimate goal—to have a connected relationship with him.

This change in my thinking about emotions did not come easily. My Connective Horsemanship training methods already worked. But they work better now because I have new knowledge that is based on research and not just what seems right to me. Knowledge is power, and power should be used for the benefit of others. I urge you to open your mind and continually seek out new knowledge. Doing so will benefit yourself and your horse.

THE SCIENCE OF UNDERSTANDING NEEDS

Understanding how horses work enables us to communicate with them more clearly. That inevitably helps our relationship with them. It's just that simple. Furthermore, a basic scientific understanding of how the horse's anatomy and physiology works—from his endocrine responses, to his flight instinct, to his nutritional needs—is a real key to creating a better quality of life for the horse. The better quality of life comes from an understanding of husbandry, how a horse should be cared for, and what is required for a horse to thrive.

2.2 A–C   *Though all are the same breed, these Quarter Horses use very different muscle groups, develop different skill sets, and perform different thought processes throughout their life. The more we develop our scientific understanding of the horse's various systems, the more accurately we will be able to anticipate and meet the horse's needs and improve his quality of life.*

The study of equine husbandry allows us to accurately discern the answers to questions like:

➤ How much space does a horse need in order to have a good quality of life?

➤ Should the horse be in a stall for 12 hours a day?

➤ How should turn-out be set up?

➤ What nutritional requirements does the horse need in order to thrive?

➤ Does the horse require certain grasses for optimum grazing?

➤ Are there additional feeds that the horse requires?

Many people who genuinely love horses want to humanize them or use anthropomorphic terminology to describe certain equine behaviors. If you take that away, they believe they will lose the elusive "connection" they want to have with the horse.

Such a delicate relationship exists between people and horses that if you start to get too scientific or too wordy, people often think they won't like what they hear and stop paying attention. I think that's why so many of the so-called "Natural Horsemanship" trainers have such a devoted following. They understand the inherent desires of their target audience and have done a wonderful job marketing themselves. They talk about "playing games with your horse," and all that nonsense. And people eat it up because they like to think that their horse can relate to them in a human way.

In contrast, I believe that taking a much more scientific look at the horse will help you have a better relationship with him in the long run, because you will work from a foundation that has a better understanding of who the horse is and how the horse works.

Don't get me wrong: I love my horses. At the same time, I have a very realistic, scientific point of view regarding how they work and react toward me. When I walk into the barn, and my horses neigh, I don't think, "Oh, they're neighing because I walked in the door and they all love me." I know better. I know they neigh because it is feeding time, and they associate my presence at that time with the appearance of grain and hay.

UNDERSTANDING GENETIC TENDENCIES

When cultivating an understanding of a horse, do not neglect to take his breed into consideration. While it is certainly true that individuals within a breed can exhibit atypical behavior, an understanding of a breed's history can be useful during training.

Breeds developed from a relatively small sampling of individuals. By default, horses within a specific breed will share the same ancestry and will have certain genetic tendencies. These genetic tendencies cause horses to respond to training in consistent, predictable ways.

Some horses are genetically geared toward excelling at certain behaviors. For instance, Thoroughbreds, Arabians, and some "hotter" breeds with a highly developed flight response may require a different training emphasis than Warmbloods and cobs. In contrast, heavier, "cold-blooded" horses, such as draft breeds, have had their flight response diminished somewhat and their bone structure and muscle mass increased through selective breeding. This has resulted in a horse that

2.3   Thoroughbreds, Arabians, and other "hotter" breeds, have highly developed flight responses. As a result, they typically have an excellent "Go" response. Their training will generally focus on minimizing the flight response and teaching the horse that not everything requires him to run away at top speed.

2.4   Draft horses, cobs, and other "cooler" breeds have more bone and muscle mass. Through centuries of selective breeding aimed at creating a horse that can pull heavy field implements for hours, their flight response has often been minimized. Many of the heavier breeds have a healthy "Stop" response. Their training will often focus on encouraging the horse to readily move forward.

reacts much more slowly to external influences, but carries tremendous power reserves.

Having a better understanding of the horse's lineage gives you an opportunity to train in a way that builds upon that breed's strengths and improve areas of weakness in order to have a more refined and well-rounded horse.

THE SUM OF ALL TRAINING

The better understanding that man has of himself, of the horse, and of training in general, the better the training process will be for all concerned.

When we focus on gaining a clearer understanding of equine motivators, horses seem to react much more fluently toward our desires and cues. Furthermore, having a grasp of science helps us to understand the horse's ways. If the horse bucks, for instance, there is a reason why he bucks. It's not because he is a bad horse, or a stupid horse, or a poor horse. He bucks for one of two reasons (excluding the fact that he may be exhibiting a pain response). Either he has not had adequate training to overcome his innate desire for self-preservation, or he has been conditioned, fundamentally *trained*, to exhibit this behavior.

A horse is the product of all his training. In many ways he's like a complex computer. If you don't push the right buttons in the right order, the computer will lock up and have problems. If you approach the horse's training from a scientific point of view, you will have a much clearer understanding of the way the horse learns, thinks, and lives. The better you understand how the horse will react, the easier your training will be because you have a more defined reason for every action you do.

The clearer you are with the horse, the more clear responses you will get from him. If the horse does not understand what you are asking of him, *conflict behavior* will result. Conflict behavior is "bad behavior." It manifests itself in horses that buck, rear, crib, kick, or bite—all the "bad" behaviors that you normally see out of a horse.

If we can make sure that our conflict with the horse is not great—if it is very, very, *very* small—and if we have a crystal-clear means of communicating, then the horse will respond positively. We won't encounter the problems normally associated with conflict issues. We will be able to break down the natural language barrier between humans and horses. Conflict will change to cooperation.

Connective Horsemanship is dedicated to increasing the understanding of both horses and humans so such conflict behaviors become a thing of the past.

2.5   *Confusion leads to conflict. If the horse is unclear about how to respond, or if his training has inadequately prepared him to cope with a situation, he will react out of instinct. Undesirable, and often dangerous, behavior results.*

A Study in Equine Communication

Horses communicate with each other in three basic ways:

- Visual—What they see, including actions, attitude, and body language.

- Chemical—What they smell and sense.

- Verbal—Sounds that, though not actual language, convey meaning nonetheless.

Because these three methods are how horses respond to and communicate with other horses, these are also the three primary ways they respond to and communicate with humans.

THE LANGUAGE OF HORSES

When discussing equine communicative behavior, I know that a lot of people think horses have language, but they actually don't. However, this does not mean that they don't use sound to communicate verbally.

Verbal communication among humans has a consistent structure. That structure lends meaning to the sounds that make up language. In contrast to actual language, horses have a basic function of certain sounds. To a horse, a sound that occurs—whether it be a nicker, or a whinny, or a scream—doesn't derive meaning so much from the actual vocalization, but is instead interpreted through the behavior that results *because* of it.

Consider, for instance, the sharp squeal or "whine" that a mare makes when another horse comes near. If the other horse encroaches too far into the first mare's territory, then the two may reach out to bite or turn to kick each other. The squeal is a threat. But that doesn't mean it's a *verbal* threat to the other horse. The accompanying attitude and actions, rather than any inherent significance, give the vocal expression meaning.

Social Behavior

Actions that happen within a group of individuals of the same species that affect the group's society as a whole are called *social behaviors*. Mutual grooming is an example of a horse's social behavior. When horses groom each other, it strengthens the bonds within the group and creates a more cohesive unit. This, in turn, enables them to stay alive more easily because a unified group is safer than a fragmented one.

Understanding social behavior is essential in order to understand horses. If, for instance, you don't understand why they become barn sour or buddy sour, or why they have the flight responses that they do, you don't understand horses. Period. Without knowledge of equine social behavior, you will have difficulty trying to explain or understand why horses do the things they do.

Humans have social behaviors as well. We get together as people because we're social beings like horses are. Humans also have an innate desire to be caregivers. We want to take care of other beings. I think that's really what helped bring horses and humans together. We both appreciate the interaction, and the horse's instinctive fear (of everything!) speaks to our need to care for him.

LOOKING FOR PATTERNS

Horses follow a *natural behavior pattern* of ingrained, hardwired things that all horses do. They all eat grass. They all drink water. They all want to be with other horses. They all display social behaviors. They all have a flight response that triggers when startled.

One of the horse's natural behavior patterns involves how conflict is handled. If conflict arises, horses want to deal with it in a nonviolent way if at all possible. To humans, the conflict resolution might *sound* violent, with lots of screams and whinnies, but at its core, horses address conflict very quickly, and generally defuse the situation without violence. Often, the situation is resolved without even resorting to physical contact of any kind.

The vast majority of horse-to-horse contact is nonphysical. In contrast, a significant portion of all *human*-to-horse contact *is* physical. The differing natural behavior patterns of horses and humans come into play and impact our ability to come to a mutual understanding.

These natural behavior patterns inevitably affect our training efforts, because (with the exception of mutual grooming), horses *don't want* to be touched. They primarily communicate with body language. Movements one horse makes have meaning to the other horses.

We, however, are very animated, physical beings. If we use any kind of training system that utilizes body language as our main means of cueing, then we are, in essence, constantly "lying" to our horses.

Consider, for instance, what happens if a trainer is standing near his horse talking with somebody, and during the course of conversation, the trainer moves straight toward the horse as he's making a point to the listener. If the horse has been conditioned to respond to the trainer's body language by moving away when he approaches, he'll do just that. All too often, the trainer will then correct the horse for moving away because at that moment, he was talking to his human companion and *not* to the horse. But the horse clearly read the "move away" cue and did what the trainer asked him to do, so he is being punished for doing the "right" thing!

Well, that doesn't make sense.

For better or for worse, our natural behavior patterns constantly come into conflict with one another. The first step toward overcoming this problem is recognizing it. The next step is to implement a training system that is consistent, clear, and that capitalizes on aspects of both humans' and horses' natural behavior patterns.

ELIMINATING AGGRESSIVE TENDENCIES

Because horse-to-horse contact is not based upon physical touch, horses rarely fight. When they do, the fights are usually fleeting and pointed. The horse's preference for avoiding physical conflict also colors his reaction toward humans.

You don't need to be aggressive toward your horse. In fact, aggression begets aggression. Aggression toward a horse is warranted in *very* few instances. Such instances generally arise when working with horses that have been conditioned to exhibit aggression from ill-informed training methods.

When working with "problem horses"—animals that have deep, ingrained aggressive tendencies—I let them dictate the severity of any conflict we have. If a horse behaves incorrectly (and that incorrect behavior has to be in an aggressive manner, such as a bite or kick, or the threat of a bite or kick), then I respond with a correction equal to the horse's level of aggression.

If self-preservation dictates that you be aggressive toward a horse, take a page from the horse's own playbook. Be very quick. Very pointed. The instant the horse responds, make sure that your aggressive behavior goes away.

Of course, if a horse outright attacks, you have every right to defend yourself. And you *should* defend yourself tooth and nail. However, true aggression toward humans is rare in horses. It almost always stems from disastrous training choices.

DOMINANT SCHOOLS OF THOUGHT

Conventional wisdom states that rank and order exists within all groups of horses. I am not so sure I subscribe to that theory.

We have put horses in a more contrived, confined setting than they are used to. Domestic horses are not able to move as freely as they should be able to, simply because most people cannot afford to buy several thousand acres for their horses to roam. Therefore, horses that wouldn't normally choose to be together are forced to exist in close proximity to each other, and fights erupt. This forced coexistence changes the dynamic of the horse's behavior in an artificial way, due to man's influence.

Some trainers advise that you "be the dominant mare" in order to command your horse's respect and attention. In my opinion, this is a bunch of hooey. A human can never be a dominant mare. We don't have the same movements, reflexes, timing, or innate understanding of equine body language and nonverbal communication.

Don't worry about where you fit in the herd's hierarchy. Just train your horse.

Our goal as trainers is not to try to communicate with horses using their own methods. At best, we would be able to achieve only rudimentary understanding. It is also not necessary to teach horses to understand the complexities of human language. Instead, we need to "meet in the middle," in a common method of communication that takes into consideration both our physicality and the horse's sensitivity.

2.6   *Horses form bonds with certain others in the herd just as we humans form friendships. These bonds can strongly influence the horse's actions and his training. Being aware of these bonds will give you added insight into your horse's behavior.*

SOCIAL PARTNERS

Just as we humans have friends, horses have certain social partners. Some horses form attachments with others; they like each other and enjoy spending time together. I have a pony gelding and a mare here at the farm that are, at times, inseparable. They appear to be "in love" with each other, as far as human observers are concerned.

Can a horse be in love? I don't think so. I don't believe the equine mind has the capacity to love like we do. But I do believe that horses

2.7   *Horses may be herd animals, but they also enjoy spending quality time with humans as well—provided there is a means of clear communication between species.*

find pleasure in being with other horses. And, spending time with certain horses gives them more pleasure than socializing with others.

Obviously, stallions are going to have certain pleasures that are associated with other horses for purely hormonal reasons. That is readily explained. Less easily explained is the equine version of platonic "friends," but such social partnerships are quite common. If left to their own devices, the little pony gelding and my mare will not leave each other's side. In a sense, they are bound together. If I am unaware of that bond, or choose to discount or ignore it, then my training will suffer from unnecessary difficulties.

Humans *can* be horses' social partners, but not to the same degree that another horse can be, simply because we aren't horses. Horses don't see us as "one of them." They see us as predators. Through conditioning, though, we can help diminish the horse's inclination to respond to us with fear and flight. We can change the horse's natural response to the point that he no longer sees us as a predator to be avoided.

In essence, that is how I help horses that have barn sour or buddy sour problems. I work to help them understand that *I'm* their social partner. I want them to know that I'm here to help them. To do that, I constantly reinforce that they are safe and that nothing bad is going to happen to them as long as I'm around.

Though the horse can learn to see humans as worthy social partners, when given the chance he will go back to relying on his own kind. Don't take this personally. Horses are herd animals. That's where they want to be. In general, my horses like to be with other horses more than they like to be with me. This only makes sense. I can't play with them like the other horses can. I can't give them the social reassurance that being a part of a horse herd can give them.

I can, however, give them different reassurances. I can make them feel like they are safe. I can groom them, and feed them, and take them out to interesting locations, and do all of the things that *I* like to do. Those things only happen when I'm present. Those are the things that I bring to the table as a social partner for my animals.

The Psychology **of Horses** 3

Why Does My Horse *Do* That?

Equine psychology is a scientific field of study that focuses on discovering why horses do what they do. Like the field of human psychology, equine psychology has many different branches, or areas of emphasis.

The training principles of Connective Horsemanship are primarily based upon two of those areas: *behaviorism* and *conditioning*.

A BASE IN BEHAVIORISM

Connective Horsemanship is built on a foundation of *behaviorism*. This school of thought posits that all learning occurs through interaction with the environment—the circumstances, objects, and/or conditions that surround the horse. Behaviorism doesn't take emotions or feelings into account.

All too often, humans try to place anthropomorphic terminology on the horse. We will say that a horse is "smart," or "dumb," or "happy," or "sad." In behaviorist terms this doesn't make any sense, because the horse's environment dictates what he is and who he is. Your horse is a byproduct of changes in his environment.

Behaviorism considers both the horse's current environment and the horse's previous experiences. Knowing the background of a horse, knowing what training methods the horse has been exposed to, and knowing where the horse comes from are therefore helpful in determining the best course of action should he be exhibiting behavioral problems.

A CASE FOR CONDITIONING

Conditioning is the process by which an animal learns to respond to a set of rules or stimuli. During the conditioning process, the animal is encouraged to do a particular action in a certain manner. The conditioning process involves *habituation*. Habituation is what happens after a behavior (whether desired or not) is repeated over and over again. Eventually, the behavior becomes ingrained and occurs without deliberate effort. When training horses, we are primarily concerned with two types of conditioning: *classical* and *operant*.

Classical Conditioning

Classical conditioning involves forming an association between two different stimuli or two events. When a horse responds to classical conditioning, he is responding to an outside source.

Classical conditioning is also referred to as "respondent" or "Pavlovian" conditioning. Ivan Pavlov, Russian researcher and recipient of the 1904 Nobel Prize for Physiology or Medicine, first documented the process. Pavlov discovered that dogs would begin to salivate at the sound of a bell that signaled dinner was on its way. The outside stimulus was the bell. Pavlov's dogs would begin to salivate in response to the bell ringing, because they associated that sound with the imminent arrival of food. The bell and food have no innate connection, but over time the dogs were conditioned to associate one with the other.

Classical conditioning is not limited to animals. For instance, we humans have been conditioned that when we hear a bell ringing, we are supposed to pick up the phone and say, "Hello," in response to that bell.

Operant Conditioning

While classical conditioning forms associations between two different stimuli or events, *operant conditioning* forms associations between a behavior and the consequence of that behavior. This is also called "response stimulus" or "RS" conditioning because it forms an association between the animal's response (his behavior) and the stimulus that follows (the consequence of that behavior).

Operant conditioning is based upon the concepts of *positive* and *negative reinforcement*. *Positive reinforcement* involves *adding* something that the horse wants whenever he evidences the desired behavior. The horse will more readily repeat the same behavior in the future, in the hopes of receiving further reward. *Negative reinforcement* involves *sub-*

3.1   *Classical conditioning is the reason that a horse neighs when you come into the barn in the morning. (I'm afraid it is not because he likes you!) The horse has been conditioned to expect that certain stimuli happen at a particular time of the day, and that set of events leads to you coming into the barn and bringing him food. While the horse doesn't have the conscious ability to recognize time, there is a daily routine—whether you realize it or not—that leads to that horse getting fed. He enjoys getting fed and associates you with that enjoyment, so he neighs when he sees you.*

tracting or *removing* something irritating in order to condition behavior. The horse then associates the behavior with the accompanying negative reinforcement, and alters his actions accordingly.

Anything that increases a behavior or makes it happen more frequently is termed a *reinforcer*. In the field of horse training, a positive reinforcer might be giving the horse a food item when he responds to a cue and does something correctly. A negative reinforcer might involve using your leg or spur pressure to make a habitual bolter run far longer than he wants to, and only removing the pressure when he exhibits signs that he no longer considers running fast something to be desired.

The frequency with which a positive reinforcer is applied is relevant to the conditioning process. Reinforcers or rewards may be given continuously, at fixed intervals, or at variable intervals. Each comes with its own benefits and drawbacks.

Continuous reinforcement means that the desired behavior gets recognized and rewarded *every time it occurs*. The reward for that behavior happens on a continuing basis. It is very easy for an animal to understand exactly what behavior is desired when that behavior is immediately, predictably rewarded every time. Often, however, behavior that was modified with continuous reinforcement will quickly revert to the "old" behavior if the reinforcement stops or is interrupted.

If the reinforcer or reward is given at *fixed intervals*, then it occurs pre-dictably, at a specific time, without fail. The reward doesn't happen every single time the behavior is exhibited. Instead, it might only happen every third time, or every fifth time. (Regular paychecks are examples of fixed interval rewards that we humans are all quite familiar with.) A major ben-efit of a fixed interval reinforcer is the speed with which the behavior that it is associated with can become ingrained and accepted as a matter of course—though this association is not made as quickly as with continuous reinforcement. A drawback of a fixed interval reinforcer, however, is that if the reward fails to occur at the expected time, the behavior that was asso-ciated with the reward will quickly cease.

If the reinforcer or reward is given at *variable intervals*, then it is dis-tributed at random times (but only after the desired behavior is exhibited). It might be given once after three instances of correct behavior, then after seven, then after two. Though it can take a bit longer for variable interval rewards to affect behavior, once the connection between reinforcer and behavior is established, it takes much longer for the behavior to revert, even when the rewards for it cease.

For certain behaviors, such as catching a horse, I'm very much in favor of using a positive reinforcer like food as a reward to get the horse to respond more quickly to the training process. In this example, negative reinforcement is more difficult to apply. However, using pressure from a hand (when working from the ground) or your leg (when in the saddle) to get a horse to move over works well—you *remove* the pressure when he responds correctly, and eventually, the horse will connect the tiniest, most subtle of touches to the request.

Negative reinforcers are often mistakenly viewed as *punishment*. Punishment is introduced after a behavior is evidenced with the intent to discourage the behavior in the future. *Positive punishment* is the *addition* of a stimulus (a sharp yank on a lead rope after a horse steps into your space) and *negative punishment* is *taking away* something the horse desires (such as removal of grain or treats) in response to a behav-ior. It has been found that punishment, positive or negative, *does not work in training animals*. Dr. Andrew McLean, and others, have noted that it makes the trainee afraid to offer a new response to a stimulus and causes the trainee to lose trust in the trainer. In addition, the punishment is often permanently associated with the people and places involved, which can lead to fear or self-preservation responses in that environ-ment, or a similar one, at any time in the future. (I discuss punishment in more detail on p. 30.)

3.2 *Giving a horse a treat when he allows you to catch and halter him is an example of using positive reinforcement.*

The reason that negative reinforcement has become commonly confused with punishment is that instead of involving the application of varying levels of mild pressure, it may—in more barbaric instances—incorporate outright pain in the name of "training." It is the cessation of pain that then reinforces the desired behavior. Because of this, negative reinforcement gets a bad rap and is perceived by some as "training with pain."

These days, most knowledgeable animal trainers—whether they work with dogs, dolphins, apes, or any other species—utilize food- or praise-based positive reinforcement training methods. Many have completely moved away from using negative reinforcement because it involves the subtraction of an irritant or unpleasant pressure to make the animal understand what he is supposed to do. I, however, agree with Dr. McLean, who says that "our job as trainers is not to deny negative reinforcement, but to encourage the very best use of it, where pressures are reduced to the tiniest of signals."

The reason I use certain tools the way I do is because I want to do the most humane thing possible for the horse during the training process. I want to apply the least amount of pressure necessary, but still make my cues as clear as possible. To that end, I do not use big bits or rope halters to get the horse to respond correctly. I also do not scare the horse into responding correctly. Instead, I use only very "light" tools. These tools apply broad, dull pressure to the horse, rather than sharply focused pressure. During the initial training phase, the horse may give a duller response at first. As his training progresses and his responses become more and more finessed, however, it is very clear to me that he is not responding to *pain* but responding to *pressure*.

CONDITIONING CAVEAT

Conditioning does not always result in positive or beneficial new behavior. *All* repeated behaviors, whether good or bad, eventually become learned behaviors. If you allow the horse to repeat an action and therefore condition himself to a specific set of rules, then that action will become an integral part of the horse's behavior.

A common example of an undesired conditioned response is seen in the horse that is a "space invader" (see p. 100). This animal has an owner or handler that allows the horse to invade the human's personal space, with the end result of pushing the human out of the way. Repeated success with this behavior conditions the horse to believe that being pushy is a good way to move the handler away whenever the horse desires—especially if the horse wishes to avoid or refuse a cue.

Conditioned behaviors develop over time. Once established, they can be very difficult to eliminate. If a horse is allowed to engage in bad behavior enough times, then it becomes *learned* behavior, or a conditioned response from that point forward.

The Double-Edged Sword

The more we understand what motivates horses and drives their behavior, the more readily we can develop and apply sound training principles to affect that behavior or modify it to suit our needs. An understanding of the horse's psychological makeup can also illuminate the negative and potentially damaging aspects of certain training techniques.

Improving our understanding of equine psychology brings the added weight of responsibility to our interactions with the horse. Knowledge can be a double-edged sword. The possibility always exists that we will use that knowledge against the horse. Some training methods commonly practiced today are, in fact, counterproductive to a horse's psychological health. Questionable training practices include *flooding, desensitizing, punishment,* and *learned helplessness.*

THE FALLOUT FROM FLOODING

Flooding involves forcing a new behavior on the horse very quickly, without much thought to the horse's well-being. Flooding often involves rapidly and repeatedly exposing a horse to a stimulus in such a way that the horse's flight response is overloaded or negated. When flooding is utilized, the horse is exhausted either physically or mentally (or both) into submission.

Very often, round penning is a form of flooding. The horse is confined in the round pen where he is forced to respond to the handler in such a way that his overall physical well-being is diminished. He is made to run around in circles, turn left and turn right, and wear his body down until he is too tired to do anything except what the human dictates.

I strongly believe that the act of chasing a horse in a round pen is possibly the most harmful thing you can do. The round pen lesson triggers the horse's fear response. Dr. Temple Grandin, noted for her work in animal welfare, neurology, and philosophy, says she believes that "instilling fear in an animal is far worse than pain." Horses are prey animals. They are the embodiment of the fear response. Since fear is quickly remembered and never forgotten, it doesn't make sense to invoke the fear response, whether in the round pen or anywhere else, in the guise of "training."

Flooding is also often employed in colt-starting competitions, to no one's benefit except the winning trainer. Any time you begin with an unbroken, untrained horse and three hours later are riding that horse around in circles, standing on his back, jumping him over fences, doing the hula-hoop, and shooting firearms while in the saddle, something has gone tragically awry. The horse has been flooded with stimuli. The end result is that he just shuts down and essentially gives up. I firmly believe that is very, very bad. Such treatment can irreparably damage the horse's perception of humans for the rest of his life. I have major moral and philosophical problems with handling a horse in this way and calling it "training."

DESENSITIZING VS. SYSTEMATIC DESENSITIZATION

The concept of *desensitizing* has grown in popularity in horse training circles. Done properly, making a horse less sensitive, spooky, or prone to overreact is an essential part of training. The way to do that is to apply pressure to the horse gradually, in such a way that the horse never "flips the switch" on the flight response and starts to move his feet. I want the horse to realize that if he doesn't move his feet the pressures will go away, the fear goes away, and the things that *create* that fear go away.

When done improperly, however, desensitizing is related to flooding. It can have far-reaching adverse affects on the horse's psyche and emotional state. This is especially true with horses that are fearful to specific objects. Instead of teaching the horse that he needs to stop his feet and stand still in order for a scary object to go away, too often improper desensitizing methods simply involve scaring the horse into moving his feet—then once the horse stops, removing the frightening stimulus. The problem with this is allowing the horse's feet to move *in the first place*.

If, during desensitizing, the horse's feet move because of the flight response, then you have gone too fast. I often see a "desensitizing" session where the horse is in flight more than he is learning to stand still and to accept that fearful stimulus. That's not training. That's using the horse's natural fear response against him.

Systematic desensitization differs from desensitizing in that it *gradually* introduces the horse to something he is afraid of. It introduces the object of fear so slowly, and in such a deliberate, nonaggressive way that the horse never feels compelled to access his flight response. He learns to not be afraid of, or react out of fear to nonthreatening objects.

Systematic desensitization is what I use to teach a horse not to fear "silly" items. I once worked with a 17-hand Oldenburg mare that was deathly afraid of flower boxes while jumping. She was a very expensive mare that had been imported from Europe. This mare would jump 5-foot-high fences with style, but if the obstacle had a flower box in front of it, you couldn't get her to jump an inch. So I did systematic desensitization. I went through the process of gradually acquainting the horse to flowers and boxes and to different related items. Over a period of time, she learned to accept flower boxes in many different shapes and many different environments.

THE PROBLEM WITH PUNISHMENT

Punishment, as we most often see it in horse training, is when you strike your horse or otherwise inflict intentional discomfort because of something he has done that you don't like.

As I mentioned earlier (see p. 26), punishment as a training method does not work in the long term. That doesn't stop people from using it as their primary training tool. The reason for this is because punishment *does* achieve the desired results, to some degree, for a brief period of time. Generally, this brief period of time is enough to convince the person doing the punishing that the undesired behavior has been changed. The sad truth, however, is that punishment is—at best—only a very weak way of training. The results punishment generates don't last for long. Unfortunately for the horse, the next time the unwanted behavior manifests, the uninformed trainer often reverts back to punishment as a means of correction. And the vicious cycle continues.

Let's examine the problem of rearing in terms of possible "punishments" for the undesired behavior. I've heard of wildly different, flat-out *crazy* things that are supposed to convince a horse he should no longer rear. Some people advise taking a stick and whacking the horse in the head every time his front feet leave the ground. I've had people tell me to break a balloon across the horse's head (evidently this is supposed to simulate that the horse has hit his head and broken his skull). Or, I've been told to take a Wiffle® ball bat and smack the horse between the ears when he rears. I've even had someone tell me to load the rearer into a trailer, then shoot him in the rump with a BB gun! ("That'll teach him!") Frankly, it is sometimes difficult to distinguish between "punishment" and outright "abuse."

I believe the train-through-punishment mentality is largely responsible for many of the problems apparent in the horse industry, because people are deliberately trying to inflict pain on their horses for doing something *the human* has determined is wrong. If the horse doesn't run around the barrel fast enough, the rider smacks him on the neck. If the horse steps on the handler's foot, the handler kicks him in the stomach. The problem with using punishment as a training method is that it takes conscious thought to connect the punishment with the undesired behavior. But horses don't engage in that sort of complex reasoning and all too often their punishment only adds to their confusion.

Instead of punishing the horse for doing something wrong, let's *stop* the behavior as it is being expressed, and *replace* that behavior with something more appropriate, safe, or desirable. That will enable us to progress in our training—without pain and without confusion. That is how I train.

LEARNED HELPLESSNESS

If an animal is exposed to constant pressure that is never released, regardless of what the animal's actions are, eventually the animal will demonstrate *learned helplessness*, and simply shut down and stand still. Psychologist Martin E.P. Seligman and his colleagues at the University of Pennsylvania formed the theory of learned helplessness in 1967. While studying the effect of classical Pavlovian conditioning on dogs, they discovered outcomes that were at odds with some of B.F. Skinner's behaviorist theories.

Dr. Seligman was doing research that supported his interest in depression. He applied a series of shocks to dogs in a variety of situations. He discovered that if at first, the dog was immobilized or in some other way prevented from avoiding the shock or ending it, eventually the dog would just sit and whine, doing nothing to end the shock—even when he regained the ability to avoid it.

The ramifications of learned helplessness in horse training are enormous. I want to remain constantly aware of the possibility that unrelenting pressure on my part can literally *teach* the horse to ignore me because he feels powerless to end the pain.

I never try to teach the horse to succumb to helplessness. I do, however, try to "train away" the horse's flight response. I want to do that in such a way that the horse *chooses* not to run, as opposed to standing dumbly because he is too overwhelmed and depressed to do anything else.

3.3   *All bad behavior has a starting point at which it could readily be addressed and dealt with. If allowed to continue unchecked, however, it can escalate into an ingrained, deeply rooted, dangerous habit that can be very difficult to eliminate.*

The Psychology of Bad Behavior

In my experience, most bad behavior that horses exhibit stems from some combination of mishandling and inadequacies in the training process. Bad behavior *always* has a beginning, a genesis, at which it could have been easily remedied if handled properly. However, if allowed to continue, bad behavior can become ingrained to the point where it is not as easily addressed or eliminated. Bad behavior is especially problematic when it has progressed to the point where it is a part of the horse's automatic response to a situation that does not generally warrant an outburst of attitude.

There are so many different ways to train a horse. Some commonly accepted ways are very flawed because the thought processes behind that particular training approach are incomplete or irrational. Mishandling and poor training cannot only contribute to a wide variety of habitual bad behaviors, but they can also lead to such problems as *lack of focus* and *handler aversion.*

Proponents of the round pen hail it as a tool that can force the horse to pay attention to the trainer. Often, however, the round penning experience results in a *lack of focus*, instead. Many horses that are subjected to round pen training sessions spend their time within the confines of the round pen in flight mode, running about in a vain attempt to leave the area. Instead of focusing on the trainer's cues in a calm, stress-free manner, they spend their energy focusing on their desire to leave, looking away from the trainer, and trying to escape the pen. Too many times, a round pen session involves repeatedly triggering a horse's flight response until the horse is too tired to run anymore. This veers dangerously toward instilling learned helplessness in the horse's attitude toward training.

Handler aversion can result when a horse's contact with humans causes constant confusion. A horse with handler aversion may not readily allow himself to be caught. If the horse *is* caught, his confusion at what the human asks him to do may be communicated in a wide variety of actions designed to make the human and horse part ways. In any case, the horse's aversion to humans is learned behavior that is directly related to improper training methods. The horse associates the handler with pain or confusion, and decides that life is better if he remains as far away from the human as possible.

Unlearning the Undesirable

Horses have prodigious memories. This can be both a blessing and a curse during training. Once the horse learns something, that knowledge stays with him for a very long time (often his entire life). When the training goes well, when we are consistent and clear, the horse will store the information he has gained indefinitely for immediate access at any point in his future. When the training is done improperly, however, *those* memories are also made for a lifetime.

If a horse has the misfortune of enduring poor training or uneducated handling, he may respond with behaviors that are inappropriate or worse—dangerous. In these instances, we must take specific steps to retrain the horse and give him new memories to supplant the old ones. The goal is to delete the horse's old undesirable behavior and to gradually reshape that behavior into something more appropriate.

THE DELETION PRINCIPLE

Once an animal learns to do something, he will never "unlearn" it. He can, however learn to do something different in place of the original behavior. Taking an unwanted behavior and training the animal to respond differently to the cue that originally produced that behavior is called *deletion*. It may also be known as "extinction," "counter conditioning," and "over training." All of these terms refer to the same thing: overlaying an undesirable or inappropriate behavior with a different conditioned response to the same stimuli.

For example, if a horse has a bucking problem, a way to delete the unwanted behavior is to stop the horse every time he starts bucking and redirect him into going forward. You're not giving a cue for a buck, so you won't allow the buck to result from the cue. Instead of bucking, "go forward" is the cue that you want. Every time the horse begins to buck, come to a stop so it doesn't become a conditioned response to your cue. Then cue again, rewarding only the "go forward" response.

If you proceed consistently and methodically, and adhere to a systematic process of deletion (called an *extinction schedule*), over time, the unwanted behavior (bucking) will no longer occur.

You can use a systematic, sequential extinction schedule to delete *any* unwanted behavior in the horse. The key to extinction is being able to ignore everything but the correct behavior. When the horse gives an incorrect response, you simply *do not reward* it. You can stop the incorrect behavior so it doesn't escalate into a learned, conditioned response, but immediately follow that with a cue that elicits the desired reaction. Only then can you delete the unwanted response from the horse's repertoire.

THE SHAPE OF THINGS TO COME

The process of changing a horse's learned behavior is a gradual one. To be effective, the trainer must methodically, slowly, change the animal's behavior through successive trials. This is referred to as *successive approximation* or *shaping*. The goal is not to affect instantaneous change. Rather, it is an incremental trend that always leads toward a more desired, targeted response using *differential* (both negative and positive) reinforcements.

The principles of shaping are present in every interaction with the horse and his environment. The human handler employs various cues and reinforcements with the intention to change the horse. Every time you work with the horse, you should do so with the intention of shaping (or reshaping) that horse to a better behavior, or a more solid response.

The more effective you are in shaping a horse's responses into correct behavior, the less likely the horse will be to respond incorrectly to the cues you give. As with all other aspects of training, consistency and clarity of cues are the keys for permanent shaping and affecting true behavior changes.

SHORT AND SWEET

When training or retraining, keep in mind that short sessions hold the most learning potential. Sessions should not last any longer than 30 to 45 minutes. Anything over an hour is excessive.

My mentor Dr. Andrew McLean of the Australian Equine Behaviour Centre (AEBC) has found that animals learn best in sets of five to seven repetitions, with short breaks intermittently between sessions. Applying this information to your training efforts means that you will ask the horse to respond correctly five to seven times to a particular cue, then leave him alone for a bit to process what he has learned. The cool thing about this is that the horse will begin to learn more quickly because you have to work both his left and right sides. While you're working one side, the part of the brain that controls the other side is getting a rest and learning.

Once the horse has demonstrated sets of five to seven *correct* repetitions, then that the behavior is *learned*. After a horse has learned a behavior, he should be able to repeat it correctly at least 85 percent of the time. All learned behavior, whether desired or undesired, has a 15 percent failure rate. As a matter of course, 15 percent of the time, the horse won't respond to something correctly. That is the norm. Never ask the horse to be 100 percent correct all the time, because that is as impossible for him as it is for you.

Combating **Conflict Behaviors** 4

Causes of Conflict

The term "conflict behavior" encompasses a wide range of responses. All unwanted negative actions, reactions, and behaviors are rooted in conflict. Two things are primarily responsible for causing conflict with our horses: Conflict responses may surface when the horse becomes confused about his training. They may also arise when the horse is in conflict with his environment.

TRAINING CONFLICTS

When the horse becomes confused about his training, his confusion often manifests as misbehavior. However, I cannot stress enough that the horse is never at fault for any of his conflict behaviors. Any "misbehavior" on the horse's part is always the rider's or the handler's fault. This simple tenet is one of the crucial foundations of Connective Horsemanship.

Conflict can arise because of opposing cues (occurring when two mutually exclusive cues are given at the same time). The most common opposing cue conflicts I see are with the "Stop" and "Go" cues. All too often, a rider asks the horse to go forward—then pulls back with the reins at the same time, either out of insecurity, poor balance, or "hand riding" (the rider thinks this is how to get the horse to "collect"). Those horses that cannot habituate to the pressure often revert to severe expressions of flight. They may buck, rear, kick, and even flip over! I consider this particular combination of opposing cues a major cause for concern as it is so prevalent within the horse industry. It is something that I would like to see eradicated completely. If it were simply a thing of the past, it could quickly eliminate many of the behavior problems that stem from consistent opposing cues.

Avoidance is another way for the horse to react to conflict. This is commonly seen in such actions as shying or bolting. The horse sees an object that frightens him, and to avoid it he moves quickly and firmly in the opposite direction. The horse's desire to avoid the object that frightens him overrides his training and causes him to disregard his rider.

Complete loss of control caused by avoidance is due to a training deficiency in the horse. It results from some combination of a lack of time spent on training and insufficient knowledge on the rider's part. Simply working correctly through these issues during the training process will minimize the horse's avoidance of "scary objects" he encounters in the future. (For specific training techniques to eliminate avoidance reactions, see chapter 10, Correcting Behavioral Problems under Saddle, p. 135.)

The embodiment of obvious conflict behavior is what I call the "Red Zone" horse. This is the horse that reacts with extreme measures. He kicks, paws, bucks, rears, bites, strikes, and bolts. He is the horse that can be counted upon to act out. But conflict can also show up in more passive "Yellow Zone" horses. These horses show a heightened sense of flight. They make their feet go faster, raise their head, hollow out their back, chew on the bit, wring their tail, stomp, or lick and chew. I explain the Behavior Zones in detail on p. 39.

4.1   *Avoidance is a common reaction when something in the horse's environment— the circumstances, objects, and/or conditions that surround the horse—causes conflict.*

MANAGEMENT ISSUES

Improperly managing the horse in his everyday life is the cause of whatever environmental conflict the horse experiences. Extreme mismanagement, such as neglect or abuse, can lead to lifelong conflict-related problems.

Environmental conflicts often differ from conflicts with the training process. Though environmental conflicts can also result in the same aggressive behaviors that stem from training conflicts, it is more common for them to manifest in the form of stall vices and pasture problems. These may include such issues as cribbing, stall kicking, weaving, and aggression toward other horses in the pasture. Horses that are at peace with their surroundings and their care will not feel compelled to resort to damaging behavior that derives from stress or conflict with other horses in their vicinity.

Behavior Zones

An easy way to categorize a horse's behavior is to think in terms of one of three "zones." Consider the colors of a traffic light, and what they mean:

➡ Green means "All is well" and "Keep going."

➡ Yellow means "Caution is needed."

➡ Red means "Stop" or "Danger."

Applying each of these colors to a Behavior Zone can be useful in evaluating the repercussions of a horse's actions.

A horse in the *Green Zone* is responsive and tractable (fig. 4.2). He does what he is supposed to do, and nothing about his current situation concerns him. In the *Yellow Zone,* the horse goes into what I call "pre-flight" (fig. 4.3). The head comes up. The eyes get wide. The nose flares. The feet start to move a little bit more quickly, taking short and choppy steps. The tail comes up. These actions are the horse's way of telling you that if you continue what you are doing, he will transition into the *Red Zone* (fig. 4.4)—and the ride will get a whole lot more fun (if you like that sort of thing).

There are two types of responses associated with the Red Zone: both flight and fight. In the Red Zone of "flight" the horse runs away, bucks, rears, bolts, and spooks. The flip side of flight is fight; if a horse cannot escape a situation, he will strike back at the perceived threat. A horse in the "fighting" portion of the Red Zone kicks, paws, strikes out, attacks, or exhibits other aggressive actions. The "flight" aspects of the Red Zone are closer to the Yellow Zone than the "fight" elements. A horse that chooses fight is in the far end of the Red Zone, and may pose a real danger to humans and other horses.

Factoring in the Fear Response

Horses in the Yellow and Red Zones operate from their *fear response.* Humans have a fear response as well. It is an internal reaction to something external that is perceived as frightening or to be a threat.

4.2   *A horse in the Green Zone is perfectly at ease, as this one demonstrates.*

4.3   *A horse in the Yellow Zone indicates that he is uncomfortable with certain aspects of his surroundings. Note the obvious tension in this young horse—he's poised to react.*

4.4   *A horse in the Red Zone is actively reacting to the fear response and is exhibiting some form of either "fight" or "flight" behavior.*

THE HORSE'S FEAR

In the wild, the horses that moved quickly in response to something that frightened them were the horses that lived to see another day. Over the years, this fear response has become inextricably ingrained. It is one of the things that every horse, no matter how domesticated, will demonstrate.

When the fear response is triggered, certain chemicals produced in the horse's body combine, pushing high amounts of oxygen into the horse's body and lower limbs. This enables the horse to move at a great speed, allows his feet to move faster, with tail flagged and head up and alert. (The horse's eyes work much like a pair of bifocals. The higher his head goes up, the farther away he can see. In order to see things close up, the horse must drop his head down.) The chemicals also saturate the horse's brain, enabling him to think clearly and very quickly.

4.5   *Targeted, incremental training layered over the horse's natural fear response may suppress manifestation of the response entirely and provide the horse with alternate means of acting in a situation where he would ordinarily flee. Police horses are shining examples of how well this can work—here, they take heavy smoke and riot gear in stride.*

The fear response fuels the horse to run for about a quarter of a mile if given the chance to do so. When the object that triggered the fear response is no longer readily visible, then the horse will stop and begin to blow through his nose, snorting and holding his head very high, looking to see if the danger is still visible.

What triggers the fear response?

Fear.

What triggers fear?

Everything. For some horses, a water bucket in the wrong place could trigger the same reaction as a bear attack.

So, the horse is one big ball of fear. The best way to combat the fear response is to overlay it with conditioned training that the horse can readily access when the need arises. These "layers" of conditioned responses can go a long way toward suppressing the horse's fear response. Failing to install them will undermine the horse's training very quickly.

WHAT HUMANS FEAR

Humans also have a fear response, though ours is much more complex, and often our first reaction is "fight" rather than "flight."

Some of the many things that can trigger a human handler's fear response include: aggression; failure to be safe; memories of injuries or dangerous situations; pain; intimidation; lack of confidence in knowledge or skill. Safety concerns are generally the prime triggers of the fear response. Fear is a means of keeping us safe.

A human's fear can undermine horse training as much as (if not more than) the horse's fear. If you have fear, the horse is going to sense it. Remember, horses are masters at reading body language. If we are fearful, the horse will see it and feed on that fear quite readily. Whereas aggression begets more aggression (see Aggression Awareness below for more on this topic), more fear begets great fear.

As trainers, handlers, and riders, we need to make sure that we are less fearful, more assertive, more confident, and more aware of how horses think. A better understanding of what we are doing with the horse is the key. When *we* understand, *the horse* understands. This, in turn, causes him to respond more quickly and more willingly to our cues, creating fewer conflicts, and making us feel more confident in our communication abilities and less fearful of the horse.

Aggression Awareness

Aggression is any action the horse takes toward a human with the intent of doing harm. I have been bitten severely, kicked, pawed at, stomped on, cow-kicked—if you name it and horses can do it, I have had it done to me.

However, I *do not* respond with aggression toward the horse (except for the two examples described on the next page). It is not possible to eliminate aggressive tendencies in the horse by beating him up with bats, or whips, or anything else.

There are only two instances when I will use aggressive actions toward a horse. If the horse flat-out charges me and tries to trample me underfoot, then I will take measures to make sure that I don't die. Likewise, when a horse is rearing up and striking straight out at me, then I will do the same thing. A horse that deliberately uses his feet and his size to terrorize a human can do a lot of harm very quickly. It is always in the human's best interest to do whatever it takes to stay safe. Fortunately for most trainers, taking assertive action for self-preservation from a long-term "Red Zone horse" is rarely necessary.

If the horse is misbehaving—let's say the horse is bolting—the last thing you want to do is beat him with a crop or some other object. That only reinforces his determination to run away as far and as fast as he can. As I explained earlier in my discussion of punishment (p. 30), when the horse responds incorrectly to a cue, subjecting him to pain because he doesn't understand isn't going to help confirm his grasp of the material. You wouldn't hit a child for not understanding his ABCs; nor should you hit a horse because he doesn't understand the cues you use to ask him to go forward. Learning is compromised when aggression enters into the training.

Bear in mind that aggression is a normal response for the horse. It is innate, built into his brain. Although rarely their first choice in a situation, all horses have the capacity for aggression if they are forced into circumstances that they do not understand, cannot avoid, and cannot escape. When all other options are exhausted, a horse will try to fight his way free from the conflict he is experiencing.

Aggression can be a learned behavior, too. Remember, *any* behavior that is done repeatedly is learned, whether it is good or bad.

Aggression is best dealt with positively rather than negatively. If possible, ignore it and work through it. If aggression in a horse threatens your safety, then be smart and send the horse to a qualified trainer to fix the underlying issues that are likely causing the problem.

Unfortunately, it is not possible to eliminate aggression from people. That is why we have wars. Human beings are just a different type of animal. We can, however, recognize our aggressive tendencies and take steps to limit them and minimize their impact on our life. It *is* possible to completely eliminate aggression from a horse. When this happens— when the human has learned to subdue his aggression, and the horse had learned that aggression is never necessary—the end result is two entities working toward a common goal, with a connection that makes their relationship much stronger and much more desirable.

Conflicted Communication

At its most basic level, the language barrier that separates the horse from the rider is responsible for the conflicts that arise in training.

One of my mentors used to say that the lesson should always be clearer to the teacher than the student. Unfortunately when it comes to horse training, all too often the teacher (the human) and the student (the horse) are on the same level of understanding. They both muddle through the training session, and then unforeseen problems arise that the human teacher does not know how to address. This only leads to more problems, and eventually, both student and teacher having less interest in completing the task at hand.

The lessons that you teach your horse need to be *clear, concise*, and *consistent*. I call this the Three Cs of training (for a more complete explanation of the Three Cs, see chapter 8, The Language of Learning, p. 77). When the rider or trainer begins to have a dialogue with the horse, that dialogue needs to incorporate these three elements.

When the horse doesn't understand the human's language, confusion results. The horse lets the trainer know that if he continues on the current path, there will soon be a parting of ways.

Too often, the language that we use to speak with the horse is what I call "Humanese." Humanese is very archaic. It uses whips and spurs, bits and chains, saddles and ropes, just to convey the simplest of things. "Go forward" is communicated via sharp pokes in the horse's ribs. A harsh yank on the horse's mouth means "Stop." Horses subjected to Humanese endure all our forms of brutality simply because of a language barrier. The horse is a captive in our land. Horses, on the other hand, speak a language that is much more refined and subtle than anything humans can come up with. Horses communicate with simple looks and body posture. Rarely do they ever confront each other with more aggressive action. They believe that all disputes can be worked out with a simple understanding of tail cocks, head gestures, and squeals of disapproval.

The problem is that not only are these two distinctly different languages, but they are also completely different forms of communication. They look different, sound different, and involve different means of interaction. No wonder we have so many problems understanding the horse and the horse has so much trouble understanding us! We don't speak the same language.

NOTHING BUT THE TRUTH

One of the fundamental drawbacks in our ability to communicate effectively lies in the fact that horses are not capable of lying. They only speak when necessary. They always mean what they say and they say what they mean. They have the perfect language for communicating amongst themselves. It is "perfect" because other members of their species never have to wonder if what one horse says is true. There is never doubt. If a horse communicates to another horse, *"I will kick you if you come any closer,"* and the other horse ignores the warning, the first horse will go ahead and kick. Afterward, he may look back as if to say, *"I told you so."*

4.6 *Horses never make idle threats, and they never lie. If a horse gives an indication that he will bite another horse, there is little doubt it will happen unless the second horse alters his behavior.*

All horses, whether domesticated or wild, tell the truth. Nothing a horse does is wasted motion or miscommunication. Every action in a horse's life means something to every other horse he meets. We, on the other hand, are not tuned in to our movements, our body language, or our posture. The sheer magnitude of our ignorance as regards these matters is very confusing to the horse.

From the horse's point of view, humans are a bunch of lying "yahoos." We aimlessly swish our arms around. We make funny faces that have no purpose and carry no meaning. Our ears are always laid back flat on our head. We are forever either marching toward our horse or skipping alongside. We are loud obnoxious creatures that say things that make no sense.

NEGLECT AND ABUSE

Abuse can take many forms. Some abuse is intentionally violent, as when a human handler allows himself to lose his temper and take his anger out on the horse. Some abuse is unintentionally damaging, as when a trainer uses crude or painful training methods because that's how he was taught to work with horses. And neglect is a passive form of abuse.

Anytime an animal is abused or neglected, an enormous amount of damage occurs in several areas of that animal's life. In addition to the obvious physiological damage, psychological damage also results.

Horses have grand memories. They can store large amounts of memories in their brain to recall and put to use later. When in the hands of competent owners, handlers, and trainers, the horse's prodigious memory is a great asset. However, when the horse is subjected to abuse, his memory can become a liability. Memories of poor treatment can indelibly imprint upon a horse's brain and affect his attitude toward training, and toward humans, for the rest of his life.

Another unfortunate thing about abuse is the long-term phys-ical damage it inflicts on the horse. When the horse is forced to endure a prolonged abusive situation, he builds up large amounts of corticosteroids in his body. The elevated rise of cortisol in the blood can manifest itself in health issues such as ulcers and chronic colic. It can also result in redirected aggression and stereotypical behaviors such as cribbing, wood chewing, and self-mutilation. All of these behaviors have a direct result on the horse's well-being.

Abuse because of ignorance can be eliminated with educa-tion. Abuse that results from anger or deliberate cruelty is intol-erable. I believe that an abuser of any animal should be dealt with to the fullest extent of the law.

Most concerning of all, we are *never* consistent. In a nutshell, *confusion causes conflict*, and we are the kings of confusing horses.

So how do you get around the language barrier? You need an interpreter. You need a system to help you identify when a horse is confused. You need a language that makes sense to both you and the horse. This is where Connective Horsemanship—a behavior-based means of communication—comes in (see p. 67).

Correcting the Conflict

To correct any confusion on the horse's part, we must first realize what communication difficulties are causing the conflict. All too often, owners and riders fail to recognize that the problems their horses are having lie squarely on their shoulders.

The horse is not a reasoning being. He cannot work through why his handler's cues are not consistent from day to day. He has no idea why there is a large chunk of sharp metal in his mouth. He doesn't understand why the saddle doesn't fit properly. He doesn't know why some cues are too strong and others are too weak. All these conflicts, and others like them, must be addressed before work can actually start on the problem those conflicts are creating.

Simplifying the language that is spoken through the reins, legs, weight, and other aids can often go a long way toward rehabilitating horses that have been stressed by opposing cues (I discussed this on p. 81). The process I use to rehabilitate any horse is not complex. It is a simple method of *error-free training*. In essence, I don't allow the horse to practice the behaviors that I don't want to see from him. I use the technique of *deletion* to tell the horse that his behavior was improper and to ask him to attempt a different response (for a more detailed examination of the process of eliminating unwanted behaviors, see The Deletion Principle on p. 34).

Through consistent communication, the horse begins the process of overlaying the old, *unwanted* response with the newer, *wanted* one. When that happens, the original conflict is over, and the pathways of communication are clear.

Eliminating the "E Factor"

Careful consideration of a horse's behavior is essential in order to determine the best way to approach problems. An accurate assessment hinges upon the trainer's ability to eliminate emotion (what I call the "E Factor") from the process.

Often, when I evaluate a horse, I marvel that the owner, or trainer, or handler remains blind not only to the problem, but to the source of that problem as well. Then I remember the "E Factor." *Emotional interference* is probably the most universal problem in decision-making. (This is true in our personal and professional lives as well. If we could only look past our emotional reactions to a situation, we would more readily see the truth and make far sounder decisions.)

Your emotions often inhibit your ability to see that the horse is simply a product of the sum of all his training. Many owners are tied so closely to the emotional state of their horses that any rational observation is hindered. This inability to separate personal emotions from the horse's behavior issues cripples the handler's ability to decipher the horse's actions. As a whole, today's "horse people" have made great strides toward a connected relationship with their horses. Yet, sometimes it seems that answers to the simplest questions such as, *"Why does my horse act this way?"* are as distant and perplexing as far-off galaxies. The reason for this is simple: we too often allow ourselves to be blinded by our own emotions.

The Root of All Issues

As I mentioned on p. 37, I believe that the root of all equine behavioral problems can be found in poorly taught or unconsolidated "Stop" and "Go" cues. The more I work with conflicted horses and study the writings of other horsemen whom I respect, the more this belief proves to be true.

All your communication with your horse is somehow related to either asking him to "Stop" or asking him to "Go." This is not an oversimplification; it is a truism. Like the adage "You can't see the forest for the trees," we can't see the truth of the problem because we allow our emotions to blind us and make us question the validity of such simplicity.

If our communication efforts are focused on asking the horse to either stop or to go, it follows, then, that any problems we experience with the horse stem from problems with our cues for those actions.

5.1   *An inadequate "Go" cue is evidenced in horses that rear or buck.*

5.2   *An inadequate "Stop" cue is evidenced in horses that bolt or spook*

Answers Begin with Assessment

So often people wonder: *Why does my horse bite? Why does my horse rear? Why is my horse weaving in his stall? Why does my horse buck? Why does my horse bolt? Why does my horse run away when I try to catch him?* All of these questions, when set against a solid evaluation program, can be answered. You must, however, know how to determine the "why." The key is in evaluating the horse's behavior. Connective Horsemanship employs a four-step evaluation process:

➡ Observe

➡ Evaluate

➡ Plan

➡ Act

The OFPA Method is the assessment technique I use when evaluating *all* horses, whether they are potential candidates for my Behavioral Accreditation Program, horses clients bring to me, or those that come in to my Fresh Start Program.

STEP 1: OBSERVE

When beginning an assessment, remember that all behaviors change when influenced by an outside force. Because you want to know what "normal" behavior is for the horse, you must neither interact nor interfere. At first, simply *observe*. Observation without interference allows you to accurately identify many behavior issues the horse has.

Environmental Considerations

If you are unfamiliar with the horse and his situation, begin with observing the horse's environment (see p. 23). Even if the horse is yours, and you are responsible for his daily care, try to look at his surroundings from a fresh perspective. Consider the general conditions of the stall, pasture, and other horses that he associates with. Sometimes, a look around the environs from the horse's point of view can identify some basic key things that need to be changed to make the horse more comfortable and more at home.

Horse-to-Horse Behavior

After you have examined the physical setup, *watch* the horse. Watch him at liberty in the pasture. Watch how he relates with other horses. Watch how he carries himself when he moves. Watch the horse when he is in his

5.3   *The horse is a product of his environment. Consider every aspect of the horse's surroundings and companions during the observation phase. Be careful not to interfere, however. Outside interference will affect and modify behavior.*

stall. As you observe, make notes about his behavior. Question everything and look for specific answers. For instance:

➜   Does the horse weave, crib, pace, kick the walls, or bite objects in the stall?

➜   Does the horse fight with others more than normal? (Any amount of conflict is abnormal in a balanced herd.)

➜   Is there ongoing dissention in the herd?

➜   Does the horse pace the fence or avoid it?

➜   Is the horse disengaged or disconnected? Is he refusing or reluctant to interact with the other horses in the herd?

➜   Does the horse have any physical tics or nervous mannerisms? Does he constantly flap his lips, swish his tail, or suck in air?

➜   Is the horse weaving at the gates or screaming?

➜   Is the horse running excessively?

➜   Is the horse herding the other horses around?

Most horses will exhibit one or more of these behaviors infrequently. Taken out of context, these behaviors may seem quite normal. Ritualistically performing such behavior, however, is *abnormal.*

If the observation phase reveals these or other indicators of stress, your next step is to isolate the stress and remove it (if possible) from the horse's environment. Often, this alone will not be enough to eliminate all behavioral issues, but it will help you make inroads toward a balanced horse.

Consider the herd dynamics as you do your observations. It is far from ideal to have stallions turned out with geldings, geldings with mares, mares with stallions, and two-year-olds with 20-year-olds. Such haphazard arrangements only invite ongoing stress and conflict. You want your herd balanced properly—by personality and energy level—so that all members interact peaceably.

5.4 *A horse that habitually engages in stable vices or other nervous mannerisms indicates the negative influence of a stressful environment. Habitual pacing of the fence line can detrimentally affect the horse's weight and conditioning, as well as inhibit his ability to focus and learn in training situations.*

Horse-to-Human Interaction

The final thing to look for during the observation portion of the assessment is how the horse responds to human interaction.

If someone other than you is experiencing problems with the horse, take the time to objectively observe how the human interacts with the

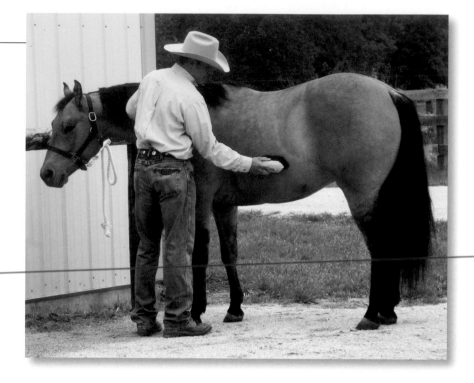

5.5 *Observe how the horse reacts to the humans with whom he comes in contact. Much can be learned from taking note of the horse's level of relaxation, confidence, and acceptance of his handlers.*

animal. Observe them in the stall, in the pasture, when tacking up, and when riding.

Constantly be on the lookout for any kind of miscommunication between horse and the rider. Also evaluate the equipment that the rider uses on the horse. Consider the following:

➤ Does the rider consistently use harsh equipment such as severe bits, whips, chains, and big spurs?

➤ Does the saddle fit correctly?

➤ Does the blanket fit correctly?

➤ Do the bit and bridle fit correctly? Is the bridle balanced?

➤ Does the horse have boots on?

➤ Is the horse shod?

➤ How does the horse react when in the rider's presence?

➡️ How does the horse react when the rider touches him?

➡️ How does the horse react when the rider leaves?

The answers to these questions can help you get a feeling for the horse-human relationship. If you are the horse's primary handler, be as objective as possible during this phase. It might help you to enlist a knowledgeable friend to help with the observation process.

The Horse as a Whole

Before moving on to the next step of the process, be sure to take a look at the whole horse. Ask yourself, "What can I fix to make things better for this horse's behavior?"

Begin with an in-depth look at his nutrition. Make sure the horse is not being fed high amounts of carbohydrates or very starchy, protein-rich foods. The horse was made to live on different types of flora—a variety of plants and vegetation are his ideal diet. He needs more hay and grasses than he does grains. If he is a performance-type horse that requires the added energy boost, then you will need to supplement with good quality crimped oats and some high-energy oil.

Next, look at the hooves and make sure that each one is balanced. You can't safely drive down the road with a set of unbalanced tires. You know your car is not going to perform well with tires that are flat. The same holds true with the horse's hoof. If the hoof is unbalanced, the horse is going to run differently, feel differently, and behave differently.

Furthermore, if the hooves are in bad shape, the horse's body will not perform optimally. There literally won't be enough blood flow through his body. The horse's hoof acts as a compressor for the blood to move up and down the leg. Without good hoof health, the horse's body is deprived of energy.

Of course, the overall health of the horse is important as well. If he is sick, if he has vertebrae that are out of alignment, or if he has underlying injuries, there could well be a physical source causing the behavioral problem.

STEP 2: EVALUATE

After a thorough period of observation, the second step of the process is to *evaluate* the horse.

Take the horse in-hand at first and work on Basic Control, Lightness, Rhythm, Line, and Connection (see p. 90), in order to see where the "holes" in his behavior or his training occur. Problems that show up in-hand will give a definite indicator of problems under saddle. Work in-hand enables you to see exactly where you should hone in under saddle, so you won't get yourself into a predicament. The indicators are always there—it's just a matter of knowing what to look for. For instance, if the horse is a little "hoppy" when you put the saddle on, then you know when you get on his back, the likelihood of getting a buck or two is pretty high. The same reasoning applies when you are asking the horse to stop in-hand. If he won't stop with just a halter, then he's not going to stop with a bridle.

Evaluating the horse in-hand gives you an opportunity to ask yourself, "What do I need to do with this horse to make him a better, more productive member of human-horse society?"

After a thorough evaluation of the horse in-hand, saddle up and evaluate his basic control when ridden. Again, evaluate his responses to the basics: go, stop, turn left, turn right, back up, and stand still. Ideally, the horse will immediately respond correctly to all these basic commands. He should respond without resistance and should follow your cues. Much can be learned, however, from the horse's behavior during the evaluation. For instance:

STAY SAFE!
_____

Please note: If you start a training session under saddle and begin to feel unsafe, you should *dismount immediately* and evaluate the situation to determine if the training should continue with groundwork or be discontinued until another time. If, at any time, a situation arises that you do not know how to handle, err on the side of caution. Don't take risks that might endanger yourself or your horse.

Neither you nor the horse benefits from a dangerous situation. Stay safe so you can enjoy a long lifetime of satisfying rides.

➡ If the horse roots his nose outward in response to a "Stop" cue, that indicates that he needs work on understanding this cue, or requires additional training to overlay the fear response.

➡ If you have to cue the horse over and over to move forward, then work is needed on the "Go" cue.

Each of these responses by themselves means very little to the average person. However, the experienced handler will recognize incorrect responses as a precursor to conflict behaviors.

Tests for Evaluating Lightness, Rhythm, and Line

The evaluation phase is also concerned with testing the horse's Lightness, consistency of Rhythm, and ability to maintain a Line. (I discuss these further on p. 72.)

When evaluating the horse for *Lightness*, look for answers to the following questions:

➡ Is the horse relaxed when he receives the cues?

➡ Does the horse respond to the cues from both bit and leg immediately and without hesitation or tension?

➡ Is the horse overflexing his neck and disconnecting the stop cue instead of slowing his feet (fig. 5.7 A)?

◈   Is the horse flexing his neck correctly and responding properly to the pressure of the bit (fig. 5.7 B)?

◈   Is the horse able to hold the correct posture for a significant amount of time, or is his strength diminished due to tension in other parts of his body?

5.7 A & B   *Dillon overflexes his neck—both to the right and toward his chest—in response to rein pressure, exhibiting avoidance of my "Stop" cues (A). Overflexing the neck enables him to continue moving forward instead of slowing or stopping his forward motion. When Dillon correctly flexes at the poll, he readily responds to rein and bit pressure (B). He exhibits self-carriage and allows me to modify and influence his forward motion.*

During the evaluation, I test the horse's *Rhythm*. I want to determine whether I can speed up and slow down the horse without any hesitation on his part. I also want to ascertain how readily I can ride the horse at a particular speed and have him stay at that speed until he is asked to change. This element of independent continuity is especially important to the hyper-reactive horse, though it is critical to the overall performance of any horse. Not relying on the rider to micromanage the speed within a gait demonstrates that the horse has a clear understanding of the "go forward" cue and that he feels no conflict associated with this cue.

To test the horse's willingness and ability to maintain both gait and speed, you must ask him to demonstrate both different gaits and different speeds. As a rule of thumb, begin a gait at a low speed. After a while,

5.8 A & B   *To evaluate Dillon's aptitude and ability to maintain a line, I start him moving along a given track (A). Then, I release the rein, and drop the cue intensity to "zero." The better the horse's Line, the more readily he will remain on the established path (B).*

progress to a higher, "medium" speed. Then move up to an even higher speed. Afterward, ask the horse to begin slowing down through each of the speeds, while maintaining the same gait.

Testing for Rhythm goes hand in hand with determining the horse's willingness to maintain a given *Line*. To test this, place the horse on a specific path. Then, drop your cue contact to "zero" and allow the horse the opportunity to make the mistake of falling off the line you have established (figs. 5.8 A & B). A horse that has mastered the concept of Line will maintain the original path. One that has not will immediately veer onto a different track once the guiding pressure of reins and legs is removed.

If the horse passes the simple tests involved in the evaluation phase, then a true connection has been made in his mind between your cues and his optimum response to those cues. You should have no difficulty progressing onward in your specific discipline and you shouldn't have too much trouble from the horse. However, if the horse fails to pass any (or all) of the tests in the evaluation, then it's time to move on to the next step of the assessment.

STEP 3: PLAN

After you have observed and evaluated the horse's behavior in a variety of situations, it is time to *plan* how to best attain the desired responses that the horse failed to perform.

One of the problems I've seen over the years is that people simply ride or train their horses without any plan of action. They just sort of poke around, find a problem here or there, work on that problem for a little bit and then get bored. They go on to something else and never see any real improvement in their horse because they don't focus long enough to make any real change or improvement. Essentially, they don't set any goals.

When I help an owner who is experiencing difficulties with a horse through the planning phase, we write down the specific goals that the owner wants to accomplish in the next few days. I use the KISS Method ("Keep It Simple, Stupid") in order to make things as easy for the horse and the handler as possible. The success of your plan depends upon this. Keep your training cues as simple as "Go" and "Stop." These are your basic responses and are the foundation from which every other response is built.

Plan each day before you go out and work with your horse. This provides a direction for you to take and keeps you from the temptation to deviate from the initial plan you set forth.

In developing your plan, define what the issue is. Perhaps the horse bolts when you get on him. Maybe he bucks. These two separate issues reflect the horse's understanding and execution of "Go" and "Stop." A bolting horse doesn't understand the stop cue well enough whereas the bucking horse doesn't want to go and sometimes stops too much.

Sample Plan *"Bucking Horse A"*

I will focus on in-hand lessons for Basic Control, Lightness, Rhythm, Line, and Connection, with a reevaluation of under-saddle work after in-hand work is finished. I will work on the "go forward" cue as that is where a major part of his problem lies.

LESSONS

Basic Control

1 *Go forward along the fence (right five to seven times correct, left five to seven times correct).*
2 *Stop along the fence (to the right and left five to seven times correct).*
3 *Turn off the fence (look for horse to respond correctly to slowing pressures both left and right sides).*
4 *Back Up (work along fence to condition horse to better stop; look for horse to take multiple steps backward; both going to left and right).*
5 *Stand Still (horse should stand still for 10 seconds each time asked; build on duration of standing still so he remains stationary until he's asked to move).*

Lightness

1 *Relaxation (horse must display all qualities of Basic Control with relaxation, which will come with a more complete understanding of cueing language).*
2 *Head-down cue (walk horse along the fence in-hand and ask him to lower his head with pressure, begin with halter and lead and graduate to bridle once horse has a cursory knowledge of head-down cue).*
3 *Flexion (walk horse down rail and ask him to stop with nose toward chest)*
4 *Flexion (walk horse in circle asking him to give his head to inside of circle and remain soft and fluid through turns; important that his body takes shape of the circle— he shouldn't remain stiff through turn).*
5 *Strengthen responses by doing each exercise in sets of five to seven CORRECT repetitions.*

When you create your plan, ask yourself which exercises will make it clear to the horse what your rein cues mean, what your leg cues mean, what "Stop" means, and what "Go" means. A benefit to this plan is that when you act to implement it, you'll know what you want the outcome to be.

When I create a plan for a particular horse, I typically have between five and seven lessons I want to teach him about a specific issue. These steps are all laid out in my program, which makes it easy to progress.

Write the plan of action down on a piece of paper. (It is very important to be able to write out your plans. I have discovered that if people *don't* write them down, then they don't happen.) When you go out to the barn each day, a written plan helps keep you very focused on the things you want to work on.

5.9 Here is a sample plan for "Bucking Horse A," who I evaluated on p. 56. Develop a plan of action. Use it. It outlines the process you have determined to follow in order to reach your goals. (For more information on Basic Control, see pp. 72 and 90, and for information on Lightness, see p. 72.)

Once a horse begins to show improvement and meet the goals that the plan was developed to achieve, then it is time to move on to the next behavior issue. Your plan keeps your training on track.

STEP 4: ACT

The last step in this process is to take *action*. Go outside, get your horse, and get to work on the plan you came up with.

All the best-made plans in the world will be worthless unless you actually go out and do them. The action portion of the assessment is the key to changing your horse's behavior. Without it, you've just got a bunch of words on a piece of paper. It doesn't do you or your horse much good if you are not actually working on what your *observation*, *evaluation*, and *planning* suggests.

"Special Needs" Horses

The evaluation of a horse in need of rehabbing differs significantly from the evaluation of a "normal" horse. A normal horse doesn't need rehabilitation. He is not conflicted. He is not at odds with himself. The conflicted horse, on the other hand, has problems, and rehabilitation is warranted in order to work through those problems.

SAFETY FIRST

When working to rehabilitate or reclaim a horse with behavior problems, remember that your safety comes first. This is non-negotiable. A "Red Zone" horse may have some behavior issues that endanger any human within his range. Take all possible precautions to maintain your safety and your welfare while working in the horse's vicinity. Do not take chances. Do not rush. Do not relax your awareness or drop your guard around the horse. Any horse can move faster than any human. Do not put yourself in a position that could allow a horse with deeply ingrained behavior issues to hurt you.

Ensuring the horse's safety is the next essential element when working toward reclamation. Take great care that you don't frighten the horse into a hostile reaction. Things that many well-adjusted horses can handle are red flags to horses with serious behavior issues. A horse that suddenly rears, strikes out, kicks, bolts in a panic, or charges, for instance, can injure himself in the blink of an eye.

Not everyone is qualified to rehabilitate a horse with behavior issues. Before you begin such an undertaking, take an objective look at your experience and your training skills. Anyone who wishes to successfully reclaim a "problem horse" should have successfully trained a number of problem-free horses beforehand. Never allow ego or pride to cloud your judgment on this point. Before you begin working to eliminate ingrained dangerous behavior, you should be able to know how to handle a horse. If you don't—if this is your first horse and you have problems—you owe it to both your horse and yourself to find a professional.

HAUNTED BY HISTORY

A rehabilitated horse is *never* free from his past. Because of the horse's prodigious memory, fear is quickly remembered and never forgotten. You can layer new responses on top of that old, fearful memory—but it will always be there.

No matter how well trained or how completely the horse responds to the reclamation process, the trauma, abuse, or neglect he previously endured must always be taken into consideration. For the rest of the horse's life, his training must first accommodate what happened to him in the past. The experiences that caused the behavior issues in the first place will always be a part of his life. You invite disaster if you ignore them.

TRAINING TAKES TIME

Remember that rehabilitating and changing a horse's behavior from one consistent action to another takes time. No horse can be "fixed" in only one lesson. You must repeat those steps the horse needs to consolidate his learning as many times as necessary before the horse is fully rehabilitated.

All behavioral issues are fixable. I firmly believe that no problem exists that doesn't have a solution. Retraining is merely a matter of how deeply habituated the incorrect response is and how much time you want to invest in correcting the problem.

Though all problems are solvable, some problems may require accredited behavioral specialists. Such trainers have been taught to deal with behavior issues. They know how to change these issues with the least amount of force. They know how to make use of the most effective method to achieve significant results in a short period of time.

PART TWO

Training for Better Horse Behavior

Where Science Meets Tradition

Connective Horsemanship® is a marriage of science and tradition. I have taken scientifically proven methods and molded them or melted them together with traditional training programs. I use science as part of my program to justify what I do. Every element of Connective Horsemanship has a basis in science. Other people have gone through the trouble of doing the research and discovering that the horse responds to certain aspects of his surroundings, his handling, and his daily routine in specific, predictable ways. It only makes sense to capitalize on their findings and structure the horse's training program to make the most of his natural inclinations.

Most other trainers haven't taken the time to mold their training programs around the basic principles of science that are available to everyone. Too many of them work off hunches. They adhere to the principle of "I've seen this in many horses, therefore it must be true." Unfortunately, that doesn't always work very well.

For instance, as I mentioned earlier, many of today's horse training programs include a round pen training process that is based upon using the horse's physical abilities against him. The practice involves running the horse around in circles, asking him to turn in and out, getting him to come and face the trainer, and finally, to follow the trainer around in the round pen. This is not a good way to train the horse to do anything—it wears him down physically while failing to engage his mind. If the horse is fairly out of shape, he will immediately start looking for the release in pressure, which is the option to stop running and stand next to the trainer. If the horse is not out of shape, however, any learning that might occur must wait until the horse has been physically worn down to the point of submission. To my way of thinking, that's not training—that's dominating. And that's not necessary.

The Connective Horsemanship training program also includes some aspects of human psychology. Though humans and horses are very different, I believe that the core part of our brains—the core part of all mammals' brains—is similar. Humans, for instance, have a flight response that is very similar to horses. In horses, however, that flight response is much more readily available to them because they are prey animals. Humans, as we all know, are predators. Incorporating basic tenets of human psychology in the training techniques helps to ensure that predators and prey can more readily communicate and understand each other.

The Evolution of a Training Program

Connective Horsemanship came about from years of personal experience. I spent years training the way I had been taught, gaining experience working with many different types of horses.

Then I got injured and was laid off for a little while. A friend of mine gave me a book written by Dr. Andrew McLean, called *The Truth About Horses*.

I read the book, and was so intrigued by the insights within it that I contacted Dr. McLean in Australia. We began a dialogue, and he eventually came over to the United States and spent some time working with me. We discussed his program in detail. His work strongly influenced the program I use today, which developed and grew out of many different training styles and much equine research.

At the same time, I read up on current equine training theories. I was particularly interested in any methods that would apply to my work with training and rehabilitating behaviorally challenged horses. I subjected every promising theory I encountered to extensive practical field application.

I've tried many methods. I've been fortunate enough to work closely with and befriend many gifted clinicians and trainers. Some are highly visible, recognizable pillars of today's equine training landscape. Others are just "regular folks"—backyard trainers with good ideas. Some training methods worked better than others, but I felt that every training approach was missing one key element.

The trainers I studied all lacked any kind of scientific basis for *why* they were doing what they were doing. Often, if pressed for the principle or the reason behind a technique, they would simply say, "My dad did it this way," or, "I apprenticed under a trainer who did it this way." Too often, adherence to tradition can interfere with advancing understanding.

What makes me so different from everybody else is that, in addition to my experience, I can back up what I do and what I teach with scientific research.

Integrating science into training hasn't always been easy. Often, I had to interpret the findings and build my own assumptions based upon my own results. Several times, I resorted to simple trial and error in order to find out if what the academics were saying was applicable, because in general academics don't train horses: they just talk about it.

My studies of both traditional training methods and scientific research have led me to focus on the horse's flight response. Everything in the Connective Horsemanship training program takes the horse's flight response into account, because that's what a horse is—one big flight response. Everything the horse does, everything he thinks about from day to day, is focused around his survival and survival instincts. It only makes sense, then, to use a training program that readily accommodates those inclinations.

One for All

A horse is a horse. Regardless of size, or type, or breeding, horses share certain inherent qualities. Connective Horsemanship works with all types of horses. It's not just applicable to stock-type breeds like Quarter Horses or Paint horses. It doesn't just address issues with gaited horses, or Thoroughbreds, or Warmbloods, or hot-blooded horses, or any other particular breed or type. It works on all horses, all the time, from Minis to draft breeds.

Furthermore, the success of Connective Horsemanship is not contingent upon the horse's level of experience. The horse can be a Grand Prix level dressage horse or jumper, or an FEI level reiner, or a backyard horse that's never been taught much of anything. This is because my program is not technically a training program. It's a *behavioral modification program*. It works equally well to:

- Modify and rehabilitate horses with behavioral issues.

- Train young horses with no prior handling or experience.

➠   Improve or elevate a "made" horse's understanding, responsiveness, and communication.

How fast and how far your horse progresses in his training depends on you. How far do you want him to go? If you're just looking for a basic trail horse, then you're only going to take him so far. You will only look for a certain level of responsiveness from the horse and will not hold him to a very high standard of performance. If, however, you intend for the horse to perform upper level dressage, then obviously you will need to have a more targeted, long-term approach toward his training.

I don't focus my training methods on a specific discipline. However, one of my first passions is dressage, because it is so precise. To ride a dressage test or to execute a movement well, you must have a clear understanding of what your horse is doing and of how you're going to communicate with him.

In any case—whether you want to hit the trails or dazzle the competition—Connective Horsemanship provides the necessary foundation. It works with every type of riding discipline because "Basic Control" teaches the things every horse needs to know. I don't care whether you're a gaited horse person, or a dressage rider, or a jumper, or a Western pleasure fan. Every horse needs to know how go, stop, turn left and right, back up, and stand still. These are the six things necessary for Basic Control in any discipline.

Furthermore, based on my work with Dr. McLean, I believe as he professes that every horse needs to know how to achieve *Lightness*. Every horse needs to know how to work in *Rhythm*. Every horse needs to know how to work within a *Line*. And every horse needs to have *Connection*. Connective Horsemanship stresses these fundamentals as part of a general-purpose training program. (Find more about this on p. 72.)

Because Connective Horsemanship is a general process, it does not focus on the higher levels of specific competitive disciplines where specialized movements are required. You can certainly use Connective Horsemanship techniques to teach piaffe or passage, or a sliding stop, or a spin. None of the advanced maneuvers are possible, however, without first making sure that the basics are known. Those basics form your training foundation.

6.1 A–C *Whatever your riding preference, whether you enjoy the precision of reining or dressage, or the teamwork of performance, or just want to hit the trail, Connective Horsemanship training techniques apply. Go, stop, turn left and right, back up, and stand still: these six things provide the rider with Basic Controls, regardless of discipline.*

The Program

Connective Horsemanship incorporates five fundamental elements as devised by my mentor Dr. Andrew McLean: Basic Control, Lightness, Rhythm, Line, and Connection.

BASIC CONTROL

Basic Control covers the first stages of a horse's education. It includes six things every horse needs to know how to do. Regardless of whether a horse's future includes dressage, reining, trail riding, jumping, or Western pleasure, every horse needs to know how to do the following:

- Go

- Stop

- Turn left and right

- Back up

- Stand still

LIGHTNESS

Achieving Lightness is the next aim of training. Lightness includes developing relaxation, flexion, and strength.

Relaxation occurs when the horse is relaxed and compliant to your cues. When the horse stops, for example, he should be relaxed from his head to his tail. His neck should be down. His nose should be in. His entire body should be free of tension or resistance.

Flexion is a way to measure the horse's responsiveness when turning either right or left. If the horse is turning in a circle, his body should bend in an arc and match the arc of the circle. As a general rule of thumb, flexion is best tested on a standard-size circle of 20 meters (approximately 22 yards) that allows the horse to move forward freely (not "dancing in place" as in a canter pirouette or a reining spin).

Flexion does *not* involve hyperflexing the horse's neck or asking the horse to bend extremely to the left and right. That really deteriorates the stop cue. When I ask a horse to stop, he should not only be relaxed, but his head should also be in a straight line; it should not be off-center. It should certainly not be hyperflexed to one side, with the horse's nose near the rider's leg. When you bend the horse's neck too far left or right, it not only causes problems with the stop cue, it also breaks down the cervical spine of the horse, causing wear and tear on his spinal column that may cause arthritis in the neck later in his life.

As a horse's training progresses, each element builds to the next. When the horse is ready to work on Lightness, for instance, I don't forget about Basic Control. I start looking for a better response to "Stop." I start looking for a better response to "Go." I start looking for a better response to all the things that the horse has learned up to this point in his education. So, *strength* primarily refers to improving (or strengthening) the horse's response to the basics he learned earlier: stop and go, turn left and right, back up, and stand still. Strength at this phase of training may also indicate the strength of the horse that is at the rider's disposal.

RHYTHM

When a horse's training focuses on Rhythm, it addresses the elements of timing, balance, impulsion, and speed control. All four of these things are very important for the horse to master before he progresses to higher levels of training.

Timing applies as much to the rider as to the horse. In order for the horse's training to progress beyond a certain basic point, it is essential for the rider to improve and control the timing of his aids or cues.

Balance—both yours and the horse's—is a part of timing. If the horse carries too much of his balance in the front, on the forehand, he will speed up. His gait will become compromised; it will get short and choppy. That, in turn, can lead to problems with your own balance and timing as you ride (fig. 6.2).

Ideally, the horse moves from back to front. The "steering" comes from the front two feet. But the hind legs are the "big engine" that is responsible for the horse's *impulsion.* A correctly balanced horse does not drag himself along with his front legs. He pushes himself along with his hind legs (fig. 6.3). During this phase of training, you pay close attention to developing the power and impulsion from the back, while simultaneously fine-tuning the steering from the front.

Once impulsion is established, it is critical that the horse master *speed control.* This means that the horse willingly moves forward in a particular gait at a particular rate of speed, and will continue going forward without deviating from that gait or that speed until asked to do so.

6.2 Here, too much of Bud's balance is carried in front of him, which will result in uncomfortable gaits, short choppy strides, and a lack of impulsion. Note that I am tipped forward, as well.

6.3 A balanced horse moves from back to front. In this photo you can see that Bud's impulsion comes from the rear, he remains light and maneuverable, with comfortable strides.

LINE

When the horse learns about Line, he gains an understanding of not only straightness, but circles and diagonals as well. He learns to remain on whatever path the rider chooses, readily exhibiting Basic Control, moving forward with Lightness, and remaining in Rhythm.

CONNECTION

When the horse has a solid understanding of the first four elemental training pieces, things come together during the Connection phase. With Connection, there is no hesitation in the horse's responses to the rider's cues. At this stage, we can ask the horse to go at a certain speed, in a certain frame, and he responds quickly, without hesitation.

At this stage, I introduce the horse to the "Connection Clock." Think of a rider on a horse as a line, extending from the horse's ears to his tail, that bisects a circle. The circle is a "clock," with the horse's head at twelve. "One" through "six o'clock" are on the right side of the horse. "Six" through "eleven o'clock" are on the left (fig. 6.4).

The Connection Clock is a tool to teach advanced body movements and to practice higher levels of control. Working on the Connection Clock encourages the horse to move through his shoulders on diagonals. It involves lateral exercises—such as the sidepass and shouder-in—designed to teach the horse to be lighter on his front end, round his back, and flex his poll. This in turn helps the horse when he performs lead changes, spins, or any other maneuver that requires him to "lift" his shoulders in response to bit pressure. To learn more about training your horse using the Connection Clock, I recommend my DVD *Connection*, part of the *Five Elements of Connective Horsemanship* DVD series. (I use the Connection Clock for buck-busting on p. 152).

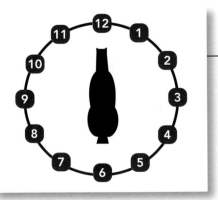

6.4   *The Connection Clock: "Twelve o'clock" is at the horse's head. "Six o'clock" is at his tail. A sidepass to the right would head toward "three o'clock," while to the left would go toward "Nine o'clock." The exercises I have developed using the Connection Clock help your horse "lift" his shoulders, round his back, and flex his poll in preparation for advanced movements.*

The Language of **Learning**

Developing a Communication System

Remember, although they have means of communicating, horses do not have language (see p. 17). They have no frame of reference for the concept. Most horse communication is nonphysical. They primarily rely upon body posture, position, and attitude. If we want to communicate with them, it is up to us to develop the appropriate means to do so.

We may want to communicate with horses using body language, but as I explained on p. 18, that dream is doomed from the start. If we, as humans, try to use our body language to convey anything close to advanced communication, we invariably end up "lying" to the horse: We are not horses. We are built differently. We don't have the same level of control over our bodies. Body language is not our "mother tongue." There is no horse-to-human translator who can help us work on our communication skills. And we are simply incapable of moving in exactly the same way, at the same speeds, and in the same manner as horses. If we insist on using only body language to interact with our horses, our limited ability to communicate will forever stunt our training efforts.

We can, however, capitalize on the horse's understanding of body language and enhance certain aspects of it to develop a horse-to-human communication system that is fairly advanced, adaptable, and that contains many of the subtle nuances associated with true language. *Pressure*, not body language, is the key. We can develop a whole multi-leveled, layered means of communication with the horse through pressure. The horse may not be able to understand our body language. In

7.1   *The vast majority of horse-to-horse communication is nonphysical. Horses utilize posture, position, attitude, and action to communicate with others of their kind. Their interactions rarely escalate to include actual contact.*

fact, it would be unfair to expect him to. He can, however, learn to understand us and respond to us through the controlled, deliberate *application* and *release* of pressure.

Pressure provides the building blocks that are the foundation of our communication efforts in the same manner that letters form the words that are the foundation of spoken language.

THE INTENSITY SCALE

Pressure works on an "Intensity Scale," beginning with 0 (no pressure at all) and escalating all the way up to 10 (maximum pressure). When training, I always start teaching a cue with a pressure level of 1, which is minimal pressure. I will *gradually* increase the pressure to 2, 3, 4, or even higher levels of intensity, until the horse responds. If the horse responds at 1, then I immediately release the pressure back to 0. If, however, the horse does not respond correctly, then the pressure intensity escalates until the horse gives the desired response, at which time, all cue pressure ceases, dropping back to 0 and instantly rewarding the horse.

By definition, the cue must have *some* pressure, or some reference to pressure, such as in the case of a verbal or non-touching physical cue given to a horse at liberty. In this instance, the cue itself triggers a conditioned response, but it still creates pressure on the horse that is released only when the cue stops—and pressure truly reverts to 0.

I continue this process of applying pressure in gradually increasing intensity and releasing it when the horse gives the desired response over and over, until the horse begins to understand that certain pressures on specific areas of his body have different meanings.

THE IMPORTANCE OF IMMEDIACY

It can't be very long between the moment you initiate a cue and the moment your horse responds. If you allow four to five seconds to lapse between the cue and the reaction, you are going to have a problem with the horse understanding the bridge between them. By the same token, there can be no lag time between the horse's correct response and the cue's release. If the release immediately follows the response, the horse is able to associate one with the other. If the release is late, the connection is lost.

Pressure must be specific in both intensity and in placement. Pressure may be applied in various ways to many different areas on the horse's body: on the sides, on the mouth, on the nose, or on the poll area, for instance. Pressure may also be applied to the area around the horse, without ever touching the horse, as in the case of a verbal cue, a whip movement, or a hand signal.

Through consistent repetition, and application (and release) of pressure, the horse learns to associate a particular pressure cue with a specific reaction. The training process continues until the horse is completely conditioned to respond in a predictable way to a particular pressure. When that happens, he totally "gets" what he is being asked to do. The more this occurs, the more the horse gains *understanding*.

Understanding is the horse trainer's ultimate goal. Greater understanding leads to decreased confusion, which ultimately leads to fewer behavioral problems and improved human-to-horse communication. The horse is always looking for a reason not to have confusion in his life, because confusion leads to flight. Therefore, the more we can develop our own language of mutually understood cues, the more relaxed and responsive our horses will be.

The Three Cs

All our training efforts are concerned with developing a language with the horse. The ideal training language is based upon a foundation of the "Three Cs." It is simultaneously *clear, consistent,* and *concise.* Each aspect of the training process works in concert with the others to form a solid, well-grounded, informed foundation upon which the horse's entire career can be built.

CLEAR

Clarity is important to both horse and trainer. The clearer your cues are, the more readily you can duplicate them, rate them, and determine their effectiveness.

If I were to start speaking gibberish, just saying words that didn't make any sense, you would quickly grow confused about what I was trying to say to you. That would cause us to have a problem in our ability to communicate. The same concept applies to the horse. Instead of a shared language of words, the horse finds clarity in the application and release of pressure.

Let's say you want to ask the horse to stop, so you take up the reins and apply a level 1 pressure on the Intensity Scale (which is light contact—see p. 78), and you wait...and you wait...and you wait...If 20 seconds go by, but you haven't increased your pressure and the horse hasn't even tried to stop his feet, then the horse learns very quickly that the cue to stop probably is *not* pressure at his mouth. That pressure, then, simply becomes something to be ignored. All too often, this scenario leads to people using big, harsh bits; though they still have problems getting the horse to stop when they apply pressure to the reins. The problem leads to other training issues—all of which stem from riders who, at the outset, are not clear about how they utilize the reins to communicate with their horse.

CONSISTENT

When you apply a clear cue and get the desired response from the horse (which means that the horse does exactly what you wish at that point in training), you reward the horse for doing the right thing and release the pressure you have applied. Regardless of whether the pressure originates from your legs, hands, or weight, or from an artificial aid such as a whip, halter, or lead line, the horse's training depends upon your ability to immediately cease the pressure when it is time to do so.

Horses learn best when they can clearly recognize the presence *and the absence* of a cue. It is not a cue's pressure that cements the horse's understanding. Instead, it is the consistent *release* of cue pressure when the horse responds that is the best way to ensure that he "gets it."

CONCISE

The definition of *concise* is "to say much using few words." The best cues for us to execute and for the horse to comprehend are concise ones: they are simple, direct, and easily recognized.

Cues cannot be complicated. If they are intricate or elaborate, they will only confuse the horse. The simpler the cue, the more readily the horse will understand it.

Cues and Cueing

As mentioned, your cues to the horse must be very simple. This is essential to the training process because you want to make it easy for the horse to grasp what you are asking of him. The horse doesn't have the reasoning ability that you and I do. Therefore, it is your job to make it clear to the horse that a certain cue means to do a certain thing.

LEG CUES

Go Forward

Let's say we want to teach the horse a cue to go forward, for example. Forward motion is the fundamental element of riding. The cues for teaching this must be simple and they must be able to be modified to mean "go forward" in a variety of directions and at different rates of speed. To that end, we will teach the horse "go forward" from pressure applied to one of three spots on the horse's side:

➥ *Spot One* is next to the horse's girth line (fig. 7.2). Pressure applied here tells the horse to go *forward from a standstill.*

When the horse begins forward motion, he must start with either one leg or the other. Since both of the horse's legs do not move forward at the same time, it doesn't make sense to apply pressure to both sides with

7.2   Pressure applied to Spot One, at the girth line, tells the horse to move the corresponding foreleg forward.

7.3   Pressure applied to Spot Two, 2 to 3 inches behind the girth, tells the horse to extend his stride and move the corresponding foreleg forward farther, faster.

7.4   Spot Three is well behind the girth area. Pressure applied here influences the motion of the horse's hind legs, encouraging the corresponding hind leg to step underneath the horse's body and move laterally away from the pressure.

both legs at the same time. Pressure from the *rider's right leg* at the girth will influence the *horse's right leg* to move forward. Pressure from the *rider's left leg* at the girth will influence the *horse's left leg* to move forward.

Which side you use to cue the horse to begin moving forward depends upon which way you want to go or what you want him to do. When you are going in a straight line, it doesn't really matter which side begins the forward motion. If, however, you know that within three or four steps you will be making a right turn, then use the right leg at the girth to cue the horse's right leg to go forward first. This is sets up the horse to make the step in the right direction in the turn.

➤ *Spot Two* is 3 to 4 inches behind the first spot; where your leg naturally falls while you are riding (fig. 7.3). Pressure applied to Spot Two encourages the horse to *move forward faster.*

When the horse is moving forward and his leg is at the end of its stride—extended as far back as it can go—a squeeze of the rider's leg in the correct spot and on the appropriate side can influence the horse to stretch forward on the next step.

➤ *Spot Three* is slightly behind Spot Two (fig. 7.4). It controls the horse's hips. Pressure applied to this area encourages the horse to move the hind leg on that side underneath his body, toward his opposite side. The horse will essentially take a step *away* from the pressure with his hind leg.

In practice, if I place my right leg on Spot Three on the horse's right side, I am cueing the horse's *right hind leg* to take a step toward the *left side of his body.*

REIN CUES

Rein cues are quite simple. Rein cues either ask the horse to slow down (stopping and backing-up are included in this) or to lower his head and bring his nose closer to his chest.

Stop
Using the reins to bring the horse to a stop is a three-step process:

1   When tracking to the right, pick up the right rein and bring it back toward your hip or toward the center of your body (fig. 7.5 A). This slows the horse's right, or *inside* (in this case, meaning closer to the center of the arena) leg with a small amount of pressure.

2   Next, release the pressure on the right rein a bit, pick up the left rein in the same manner, and ask the horse to slow the left, or *outside* leg (fig. 7.5 B).

3   Once the outside leg starts to slow, then pick up the right rein again and cue the horse to slow the inside leg to a stop (fig. 7.5 C). The outside leg should come to a stop immediately after that. You shouldn't have to add more pressure to the horse's head or mouth, because you hold that outside pressure until he stops.

Back Up

The back-up cue is nothing more than an extension of the stop cue. Let's assume you have asked for a stop using the three-step process I just described. To back up instead of stop, increase the rein pressure a little bit on the third and final step. This cues the horse to pick up the leg he just stopped and move it *backward*, away from the rein pressure.

As soon as the horse takes a step back with his right foreleg in response to pressure from the right rein, release the rein pressure. Then pick up the left rein and give the horse a cue to take a step back with the left foreleg. To add pressure to the left rein, if necessary, move your left hand back toward your navel and below your beltline.

Head Down

The key to the head-down cue is that one of your hands goes higher than the other. The inside hand (meaning "inside" the horse's bend—usually toward the middle of the circle or arena) is raised and the outside hand moved back. This motion encourages the horse to drop his head.

To correctly execute the head-down cue, move your inside rein up toward the midline of your body, below your chest but above your navel. At the same time, move the outside rein backward toward your hip. As soon as the horse begins to drop his head, immediately release the rein pressure on both sides (figs. 7.6 A–C).

When cueing for "head down," make sure that the horse does not slow his feet, but instead simply drops his nose. For that to happen, the pressure on the horse's mouth must differ from the pressure applied when asking for a stop. Consistently apply clear and concise rein cues—up on one side, and back on the other—until the horse understands that when he feels that type of pressure on his mouth, he should drop his head while keeping his feet moving.

7.5 A–C *I apply pressure first to one rein, bringing my right hand toward my hip, to slow the legs on the corresponding side of Dillon's body (A). I follow with similar pressure on the left rein, to slow the legs on the other side his body (B). I finish with pressure on the right rein again, slowing Dillon's legs to a complete stop (C).*

COMBINATION CUES

Turns and Circles

Slowing or stopping, and dropping the head down, are the *only* two things we use the reins to ask the horse to do. Bear in mind that steering control is in the horse's front legs. The back legs are his propulsion.

Asking the horse to turn left or right simply involves telling him to take smaller steps on the inside of the intended turn or bend, and bigger steps on the outside. To do that, you must time the cue for when the horse's inside front leg is extended all the way back. Then, pick up the inside rein *as the inside front leg begins to move forward*. This cues the horse to take a smaller step.

7.6 A–C   To ask Dillon to drop his head, I raise my inside hand (here, my right) high, moving the corresponding rein up toward the center of my body (A). Simultaneously, I move my outside hand (my left) and rein back toward my hip (B). As soon as Dillon's head drops, I instantly release the rein pressure back to "zero" (C).

At the same time, slightly increase the pressure on Spot Two (see p. 83) with your outside leg. You have already said "Slow down" to the inside front leg with rein pressure, which results in that leg taking a smaller step. If you simultaneously encourage the outside foreleg to take a longer step forward, then the horse will turn in the desired direction.

TARGETED REPETITION

When training the horse to respond to any cues (whether that includes slowing down, dropping his head, or turning), it is important to not only cue correctly, but to repeat the cue enough times for the horse to learn what it means, and to teach him to respond properly.

A cue that a horse learns on one side or going in one direction doesn't necessarily transfer to a cue he understands on the other side or going in the other direction. Whenever a horse learns something new, *both* sides of his brain must be taught. You can say to the horse: "Go to the right. Go to the right. Go to the right. Go to the right. Go to the right," and the horse may do that five times correctly. Once the horse correctly goes to the right five to seven times (see p. 35), then you can stop, give the right side a break and work on training the left. Then you can say to the horse, "Now go to the left. Go to the left. Go to the left. Go to the left. Go to the left." While the left side is learning, the right side is processing what it has just learned.

Remember, when training, you are always looking for five to seven *correct* repetitions from the horse. The more correct repetitions you can get out of the horse, in sets of five to seven, the more quickly the horse will learn. If, by chance, the horse makes a mistake during a set of training repetitions, stop the horse, and begin the process over again, starting back at "zero."

This technique of teaching through targeted repetition is what makes me successful when I go to farms and work with other people's horses. Because of it, I can very clearly and quickly tell a horse, "This is the right response. I am going to give you a break, and you think about it for a second. While you're thinking about it, I am going to go to the other side and teach it the same thing." Short sets of correct repetitions make a very quick process of training horses to go left or right, to stop, to go forward, to back up, or to do whatever else you ask of them.

In-Hand **Training** 8

Everything Interconnects

In-hand problems are problems that happen when the rider's two feet are on the ground. Some, such as kicking, rearing, striking, and biting, are more dangerous than others. I call those the "Famous Four." Some combinations of these problems—rearing up and striking out, for instance, or charging the trainer with ears flat and teeth bared—are so dangerous that I would never encourage the average owner or handler to work around such a horse. Most horses do not exhibit deeply ingrained, dangerous behavior problems such as these, and those who do should be left to the care of competent professionals.

Many horses, however, show signs of minor in-hand behavior issues. These should concern the average rider or owner because every behavior leads to another. If left unattended, minor problems grow into major difficulties. I think of behavior issues as being akin to the story of the Dutch boy who put his finger in a dike that had a small hole in it. To the uninformed, a little hole that lets in a tiny trickle of water is no big deal. But the boy knew that given enough time, the water would compromise the entire structure, and the wall would collapse under pressure. The same thing will happen with minor behavior problems. Given enough time, they'll add up.

Where horses are concerned, everything leads to something else. Every aspect of their life and their attitude is interconnected. Everything from your work on the ground transfers to your work in the saddle. If your horse behaves well on the ground, chances are he will behave well

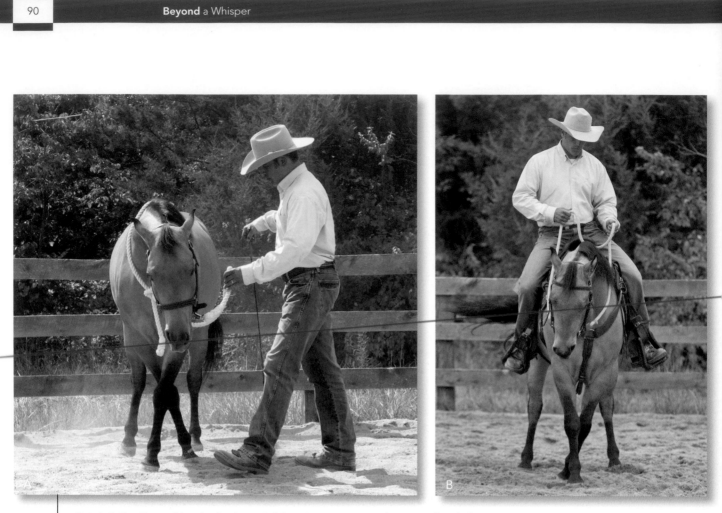

8.1 A & B   *Everything in the horse's life is interconnected. How willingly he responds to cues on the ground has a direct relationship to how he responds to similar cues under saddle. Here, Dillon demonstrates the sidepass.*

under saddle (figs. 8.1 A & B). If a horse is not responsive in-hand, he will be less responsive under saddle.

Revisit the Basics

Basic Controls—go and stop, turn left and right, back up, and stand still— are the building blocks for all your training efforts. In addition, teaching the horse to ignore distractions in a controlled environment is an important part of his education.

Ignore these basic skills at your own peril. Before you try to eliminate a specific unwanted behavior problem, spend some time revisiting the basics. They hold the key to your training success.

TRAINING TOOLS

You don't need fancy tack or specialty equipment to train horses. The following readily available tools are the only things I use to fix most common in-hand behavioral issues:

- ➤ A contained area with a *solid fence*. A round pen or a small arena that doesn't have any wire works well. (Note: The use of a round pen as a safe fenced-in area to work in is acceptable. I've already mentioned my personal views on popular "round penning" training techniques—see p.29.)

- ➤ A 3-foot dressage whip.

- ➤ A 10- to 12-foot cotton lead rope.

- ➤ A flat leather or nylon web halter.

8.2 Basic training tools include a flat halter, cotton lead, a dressage whip, and a safe working environment. These are the only tools you need to train your horse.

GO AND STOP

Begin your work in-hand with simply teaching the horse to go when you ask him to and to stop willingly. Be sure to work in a safe, controlled environment free of wire fencing or other hazards (see sidebar, p. 91).

1   With the horse haltered and with the cotton lead attached, begin on the rail, with the horse next to the fence, as if you're about to start tracking to the left.

2   Stand just in front of the horse's head, facing his tail. Hold your 3-foot dressage whip in your right hand. Place your left hand 6 inches below the snap on the lead rope. Hold the lead rope with your thumb up and your pinky finger down. Drape the excess lead rope from right to left over the horse's neck or shoulder area, or tie a quick-release knot to help keep it in place (fig. 8.3).

8.3   *I stand on the rail with Dillon, tracking to the left. I'm facing his tail with the lead in my left hand and the dressage whip in my right.*

3   With your right hand, place the dressage whip up against the horse's left side at the girth line. Begin walking backward and slowly start to tap the horse at Spot One (see p. 81). Remember the Intensity Scale (see p. 78). Start with a pressure of 1 and tap the horse very slowly and lightly at first.

8.4   *I tap Dillon at Spot One, gradually building in intensity until he takes a step forward with his left foreleg. I immediately stop tapping when he responds. I continue to walk backward as he moves forward.*

Increase the speed and intensity as necessary until the horse begins to move forward.

The horse should move his *inside (left)* foreleg forward first. That left leg has to start first if the horse responds to the cue correctly (fig 8.4). If the horse begins with the *right* leg, immediately stop cueing. To *delete* that response (p. 34), add pressure to the halter, moving your left hand toward the point of the horse's shoulder. Ask him to step back to square one, then resume the original tapping cue.

4   Once the horse begins to move forward with the correct leg, stop tapping. Put your hand in a "neutral" position and apply *no* pressure (a "zero" on the Intensity Scale) on the lead rope.

5   Let the horse take four or five steps. As he does, walk backward beside him, taking care to remain at his neck or head area. Do not fall out of position and end up near his shoulders or beside his barrel.

6   After four or five steps, increase pressure on the halter and lead rope (moving your hand toward the point of his shoulder, and beginning at the bottom of the Intensity Scale) and ask the horse to stop.

WHAT SHOULD I DO WHEN...?

PROBLEM:
My horse raises his head when he stops in Step 6.

SOLUTION:
During this training phase, it doesn't matter how the horse stops, as long as he *stops.* He can have his nose up, nose out, head up, head down, he can even push a little on you. For now, all that matters is that the horse stops his feet. The only thing we are focusing on at this point is the "go."

7   Repeat Steps 1 through 6, five to seven times correctly, until the horse takes that initial forward step with the correct leg every single time. Then change directions and teach the "go forward" cue to the horse's right side.

WALK THIS WAY...

The reason I walk backward beside the horse is because I want to know everything the horse does, the moment he does it. If my back is to the horse, and I am walking forward, I cannot see when the horse begins to do something incorrectly. The time to correct a problem is *in its beginning*. I want to be able to instantly spot a problem in the making and correct it before the horse commits to it.

For this reason, it is essential that the in-hand training area be as controlled a place as possible. I prefer to work in a paddock (or round pen) that has a nice, solid fence with no wire or other hazards.

There will come a time and place in the training when I start walking forward rather than backward, but in the early stages of getting the basics perfected, I watch the horse instead of where I am going. If you don't feel comfortable or safe walking backward while working your horse in these early stages, then find someone who can help you lead the horse while you watch him.

TURN LEFT AND RIGHT

Once the horse will go and stop willingly and with *Lightness* (see p. 72), it is time to work on turning left and turning right in-hand.

1   Stand at the horse's neck in the same position as for the Go and Stop exercise (see p. 92). Ask the horse to move forward, tracking left along the rail, as you walk backward, with your left hand on the lead rope and your right hand holding the dressage whip.

2   Stop your feet from moving backward and take tiny little steps around in a circle, inviting the horse to follow your lead. Move your left hand back toward the point of the horse's shoulder with enough pressure so

he *slows down* the inside front leg. (The horse is *not* to stop moving his leg—just slow it.) Use pressure of only 1 or 2 on the Intensity Scale. Apply the pressure only when the inside (left) front foot is all the way back at the end of a stride, and is about to take a step forward. This tells the horse, "Take a smaller step…take a smaller step…take a smaller step" (fig. 8.5).

8.5   *I've slowed my feet and stepped in a tiny circle, inviting Dillon to turn off the rail and follow. (I'll stay in the center of the circle as he continues walking around me.) The pressure I put on the lead rope (back toward the point of his shoulder) is just enough to ask Dillon to slow his inside leg, which results in him turning in a circle. I hold the dressage whip in a "neutral" position, as he is moving forward willingly.*

3   Release the pressure as soon as the horse has taken the first "smaller" step. Reapply it when his inside foreleg is extended all the way back again. Cue in this manner all the way around in a circle. Think of yourself as a post in the ground spinning around with the horse circling around you.

4   Circle to both the left and the right.

5   Once a horse has finished a circle and comes all the way around to the rail again, walk backward a couple of steps and review "Stop" and "Go forward." Repeat the process correctly in each direction five to seven times.

8.7 *Standing quietly when told is an important lesson for every horse to master. This serves him well when tied, when groomed, when trailered, and in countless other areas of his working life. Dillon demonstrates this skill perfectly—to prove the point, I let the lead hang loose and rest my hands in my pockets.*

girth line (Spot One—see p. 81) and move him forward, again to where he started. Turning shouldn't be a big problem, because you're working along the fence line, but if he starts to turn left and into the middle of the arena, apply pressure to the lead rope and put him straight on the track again.

Whenever the horse moves out of position, put him back in place and repeat "Stand" or "Whoa." Do this until the horse learns to quietly and obediently stand still when asked.

IGNORE DISTRACTIONS

Once the horse has mastered basic maneuvers in-hand—when he will go, stop, turn and back up with Lightness, and will stand still when asked—it is time to improve his ability to focus on the tasks presented to him. Add some obstacles to your arena. Be creative and have fun—here are some easy-to-implement suggestions (fig. 8.8):

- Put a hay bale out, then walk the horse around it.

- Erect cavalletti. Walk him through, beside, over, and around the obstacles.

- Lay swimming pool "noodles" on the ground and walk over, beside, and around them.

8.8 *Maintain your original position while exposing the horse to a variety of obstacles. Encourage him to focus on you amidst distractions.*

➜ Erect 4-foot posts in the ground, drill holes in them, and thread swimming pool noodles into the holes to make a walk-through obstacle.

➜ Set buckets full of water, blankets, or flower boxes on the ground and walk around and among them.

Maintain your original position through the "obstacle course." Continue facing the horse and walking backward. Your techniques should not change—your instructions should be the same—*clear, consistent,* and *concise*—as they were when you worked your horse on the rail.

Training in Stages: The Station Game

I believe that you can train a horse to do anything, and to accept anything, if you gradually go about the training in nonthreatening, sequential stages. I call this sequential training method "The Station Game."

The Station Game is more a methodology than a step-by-step, "Do this, then do that" recipe. It involves exposing the horse to a series of cir-

WHAT SHOULD I DO WHEN...?

PROBLEM:
My horse speeds up through the obstacle and gets pushy.

SOLUTION:
If, at any time, the horse begins to charge through an obstacle, simply push your hand that holds the lead rope toward the point of the horse's shoulder. The pressure this causes on the halter shuts off the horse's forward motion and tells him, "Just stop." Back him up immediately and try navigating the obstacle again. Continue with this process until the horse has successfully navigated the obstacle at least five to seven times. As you walk through a variety of obstacles and reward desired behavior, you will soon realize that the horse no longer pushes into you.

8.9   *A horse can be trained to accept almost any situation. The key to such training is to do it in stages, gradually exposing the horse to more and more of what you eventually want him to accept.*

cumstances that gradually take on more and more characteristics of the final, desired outcome—but doing it in such a way that the horse doesn't violently react and calmly accepts each permutation of the situation.

SOLVING IN-HAND BEHAVIOR PROBLEMS WITH THE STATION GAME

On the pages that follow, I have identified four of the in-hand behavioral problems I most commonly encounter. For each one, I assume that the handler has already spent considerable time working on the Basic Controls (see p. 90) and itemize a systematic way to eliminate the unwanted behavior that builds upon what the horse already knows. Bear in mind that these are not overnight fixes for these behavioral issues. In some instances, depending on how skittish or poorly trained the horse is, the process can take days.

Retraining the "Space Invader"

"Space invaders" are those horses that walk into your space, walk on top of you, or blast past you. They have no manners. As you walk up to a gate, the "space invader" runs through the gate with you. He wants to take control of the situation and tends to push people out of the way (fig. 8.10).

WARNING: DO NOT SKIP STEPS!

If your horse exhibits one or more of the following in-hand issues, you may be tempted to begin *here*, rather than with establishing Basic Control (see p. 90). That would be like sending a child who is having difficulty mastering classroom material into the next grade. Frustration on all sides—both teacher and student—would result, and very little learning would take place.

Be sure that you and your horse have spent some time mastering the Basic Controls *before* you progress to the exercises that follow to eliminate specific problem behaviors. This not only sets up your horse for success, but also immeasurably streamlines the training process.

8.10 *A horse that crowds the handler is generally reacting out of fear, and allowing the situation, rather than the handler, to dictate his actions.*

"Space invaders" are nothing more than fearful horses. Frequently, the fear response is evident or the horse is executing a refusal (also out of fear). When the horse is heavy and pushy about stopping, or wants to plow forward, it is time to ask him to stop with *Lightness* (see p. 72). He needs to learn to stop without probing his head through the pressure you apply to the halter. To accomplish this:

1 Apply light pressure (see the Intensity Scale on p. 78) slightly *upward* with your left hand on the lead rope when first asking the horse to stop. Then, *add* pressure toward the point of the horse's shoulder (fig. 8.11).

2 If the horse doesn't stop immediately, then very *quickly* and very *sharply* move your hand holding the lead rope upward, from the shoulder toward the horse's ear—almost straight up in the air. This will stop the horse's feet very quickly (fig. 8.12).

3 Ask the horse to go. After a few steps forward, stop him and have him stand still. Pet him while he's standing quietly. Repeat Steps 1 through 3 until the horse stops quickly, responsively, and with Lightness.

Remember, always give the horse the option of giving you the correct response the first time you ask. Start at "zero." Cue with a pressure of 1 on the Intensity Scale. If that doesn't get an immediate response, and if the horse doesn't stop promptly and lightly, then increase the pressure to 2, and then move to 3, 4, 5, 6, 7, 8, 9, 10. Progress from a pressure of 3 to 10 very quickly and concentrate on getting the horse to stop almost immediately.

If you focus on this training and follow these simple steps, you will make great strides with your horse. With consistency and practice as part of your approach, you should not have to go back and fine-tune anything afterward.

Dealing with Head Shyness

Like "space invading," head shyness in horses is a fear issue. When dealing with a head shy horse, it is important that you take care *not* to scare the horse anymore than he already is. Sometimes great damage is done in the name of "training."

Head shy horses are products of their own natural fear response. The goal when working with a head shy horse is to get him to no longer trigger that fear response when faced with certain stimuli—such as a human's hand touching his ears (figs. 8.13 A & B).

When working with a head shy horse, remember the Behavior Zones (see p. 39). A horse that is extremely head shy, fearful, and frustrated is in the Red Zone. If pushed too far, his fear could cause him to become aggressive toward his handler.

WHAT SHOULD I DO WHEN...?

PROBLEM:
I followed Steps 1 through 3, and things improved for a while, but my horse always gets sloppy and begins to crowd me again.

SOLUTION:
Capitalize on what you have already taught him (see Basic Control, p. 90). As soon as the horse starts to push forward into you, move your hand holding the lead rope up toward the top of his withers. Then, with the same hand, trace a half-circle toward his ears, and "push" him away from you.

8.11   *I apply light pressure when first cueing Dillon to stop. I direct the pressure from the lead rope slightly upward and toward his shoulder.*

8.12   *When Dillon doesn't stop his feet upon my cue, I raise my hand holding the lead rope sharply in the air. If this kind of correction is warranted, it must be done very quickly. Stop that horse. Give him a reason to make it worth his while to stop his feet.*

WHAT SHOULD I DO WHEN...?

PROBLEM:
My horse has a long history of being pushy. He just doesn't pay much attention to my cues with the halter and lead rope.

SOLUTION:
With some long-term, habitual "pushers," you may have to take the dressage whip and tap the horse on the foreleg (the part of the leg from the knee to the chest) during initial retraining to escalate the pressure as you counter the incorrect behavior and ask him to step back out of your space. The most important thing is to simply continue with the process. Depending upon your consistency, and on how deeply ingrained a horse's "pushiness" is, it should take anywhere from two to four weeks before the horse no longer thinks of "invading" your space.

8.13 A & B *The head shy horse reacts out of fear and enters the Yellow Zone (see p. 39) very quickly, in an effort to avoid having any human contact with his head or ears (A). With targeted training to delete the fear response, the horse will accept having his head and ears touched while remaining safely and comfortably in the Green Zone (B).*

Your goal is to work on the horse's aversion to having his head touched without bumping him out of the Green Zone. You *do not* want the horse to go into the Red Zone—flinging his head into the sky, charging forward, and possibly rearing up or striking out. You also do not want the horse to go into the Yellow Zone, where he grudgingly endures being touched, but hates every moment of it and constantly looks for an escape. You want to keep the horse in the Green Zone the entire time you are training him.

Training the head shy horse relies on using the Basic Controls to move the horse forward, to stop him, and to have him stand still. It also utilizes the head-down cue.

"HEAD DROP"

Teaching the horse to put his head down on cue can be an invaluable training asset. (Note: I discussed using "head down" when in the saddle on p. 84. This is a different cue.) To condition a horse to drop his head on cue when working him in-hand, first review going forward and stopping (see p. 92).

1   When asking the horse to stop, simultaneously apply pressure to the lead rope in a *downward* fashion, toward the horse's feet. This asks the horse to drop his head (fig. 8.14).

2   As soon as the horse drops his head even the smallest amount—a microcentimeter is enough—release *all* pressure on the lead line and halter.

3   Add pressure if the horse raises his head at all. As soon as he moves his head downward again, release the pressure.

4   Repeat this simple process over and over, so your horse's head is held progressively lower. At some point, he is not going to want to put his head any lower. When that happens, place your hand behind his ears, if you can, and apply light pressure there until he drops his head another fraction (fig. 8.15). If you can't get near the horse's ears yet at this stage of the training, then continue adding pressure to the lead rope and halter. Although the results won't happen as quickly, if you remain patient and continue putting more pressure on the lead rope, he will eventually drop his head down where you want it.

8.14   *While stopping, I apply downward pressure to the lead rope to encourage Dillon to lower his head.*

8.15   *I apply light pressure behind CJ's ears to cue for a "head drop." I'll release the pressure the instant he responds, even the slightest bit.*

8.16 *Holding the lead rope and whip in my left hand, I lightly pat the top of CJ's neck with my right hand, over and over until he stands comfortably, relaxed and unbothered by the action.*

The entire "head drop" training process has a snappy rhythm or cadence to it. It has to be very much in time—the pressure increases as the horse raises his head and goes away when he lowers it. The rhythm of pressure increasing and decreasing has a direct correlation to the horse's response to the head-down cue. Remember, the best reward for a job well done is the complete release of pressure.

THE STATION GAME—HEAD SHY EDITION

Once the horse will put his head down every single time you add any kind of pressure to the halter, or behind his ears, then it's time to play the head shy version of the Station Game.

1   When tracking left, stop the horse and ask him to stand still. Hold the lead rope with your left hand, and place your right hand on top of his neck or crest. Take it off...put it on...take it off...put it on. Do this over and over— far more than the five to seven repetitions we've used as a standard up to now. Think of lightly "patting the horse to sleep." Continue until the

8.17 A & B   *I slide my hand up and down CJ's neck, gradually nearing the ears and then backing away down to the withers. I want him to remain relaxed during the entire process.*

horse just stands there with a foot cocked, his head down, totally relaxed, and completely indifferent to what you are doing (fig. 8.16).

2   Now move your hand up the horse's neck a little bit, and then slide it back down. Move it up toward his ears; then slide it back down toward his withers. Repeat until your horse responds correctly five to seven times in a row.

3   When the horse *is* responding correctly—when he is standing still, with his head down, relaxed—then move your hand even closer to his ears. Slide it up; then slide back down to the withers...slide up toward the ears, then back down to the withers. Do five to seven correct repetitions (figs. 8.17 A & B).

4   When you can get your right hand almost to the horse's ears without any sign of a problem, then move your attention to the front of the horse. If you are on the horse's left side, hold the lead rope in your right hand and place your left hand on the horse's nose, if he will allow it. (Reverse the scenario when standing on the right side of the horse.)

WHAT SHOULD I DO WHEN...?

PROBLEM:
My horse was fine until we reached Step 4, but he won't let me touch his nose.

SOLUTION:
If the horse will not tolerate you placing your hand on his nose, then try gently touching him right between his eyes on his forehead. Do this very lightly and very quickly—remember the cadence you established on his neck (see p. 107): touch, off, touch, off, touch, off, touch, off. Repeat this smoothly, consistently, and rhythmically until the horse stands in total relaxation for the whole procedure. Then go back and try Step 4 again, touch his nose, and continue on from there.

8.18   *I stand on CJ's right side, holding the lead rope in my left hand. (Note: I have set the whip down for this step.) I move my right hand lightly all over his face. I will do this until I can touch his head completely—from his forehead down to his muzzle, under his chin, around his eyes, and on his cheeks.*

**WHAT SHOULD
I DO WHEN...?**

PROBLEM:
My horse keeps flinging his head up in the air when I try to touch him.

SOLUTION:
Any time the horse brings his head up, add downward pressure to the lead rope and ask the horse to drop his head again, as you taught him before beginning this process (see "Head Drop," p. 105). Make sure your other hand remains on the horse, even when he raises his head. If your hand "releases" when the horse moves his head up, he will learn to fling his head up in order to escape being touched. Instead, encourage him to drop his head back down even with or lower than where he started.

Gently move your hand around on the horse's face. Gradually move your hand onto spots that make him uncomfortable, but always move away from them and back to "safe spots" before the horse triggers his fear response (fig. 8.18).

5   Stand on the horse's left side near his head, facing him. Loop the excess lead rope over his neck or shoulders. Move your hand up and down his face, petting him softly. Very quickly, move your hand up over the horse's ears *without touching his ears* and continue down his neck, rubbing his neck all the way down to the withers (figs. 8.19 A–C). Then walk away from the horse for a moment. (Note: This is where it is important he knows how to *stand still* until otherwise cued—see p. 96.)

Return, and do the entire procedure again: Walk up to the horse. Pet him very lightly on the face. Move your hand up quickly over his ears *without touching them*. Place your hand back down on his neck and slide it all the way down to the withers. Repeat over and over and over. This exercise allows the horse to feel pressure, feel it leave, and then feel it come back again without ever frightening him or hurting him.

6   Do the whole process again, but now allow your hands to just brush across the horse's ears. Do this multiple times until the horse ignores it and stands relaxed.

7   Next, rub the horse's head with your hand. Move on to rub his ears. Move on to rub his neck, and continue on to his withers. Return to rub his head and repeat the sequence: forehead-ears-neck-withers...forehead-ears-neck-withers. Continue until the horse allows you to do this sequence five to seven times in a row while he stands with his ears, head, and neck remaining level with his withers.

8   Next, move your hand from the horse's withers to his ears. When you get to the ears, go back and forth over the ears *very slowly*. Slow your hand down until you are "holding" the horse's ears, while he stands relaxed and unconcerned (fig. 8.20).

ADDING PROPS

Next, go into your barn or your tack room, and find a wide variety of items to use as props in the "greater-than-less-than game." Make sure there is nothing sharp or pointed—nothing that could harm the horse in any way.

8.19 A–C *Quickly, calmly, I move my right hand from CJ's face, up and over his ears **without touching them**, and down his neck. Then I will leave him briefly to absorb the lesson, before returning and repeating the procedure.*

8.20 *If trained in stages using the Station Game, eventually the head shy horse will come to accept having his ears touched with no adverse reaction, like CJ demonstrates here. It just takes a little patience.*

8.22 A & B   *I accustom Dillon to having his front and hind legs touched in stages. Using the dressage whip, I touch him in one spot, then move away. Touch him again…move away. I gradually touch him more and more, for longer and longer, until Dillon is relaxed and unconcerned about having his legs rubbed with the whip. Note: I encourage you to have a second handler hold your horse as you go through these steps.*

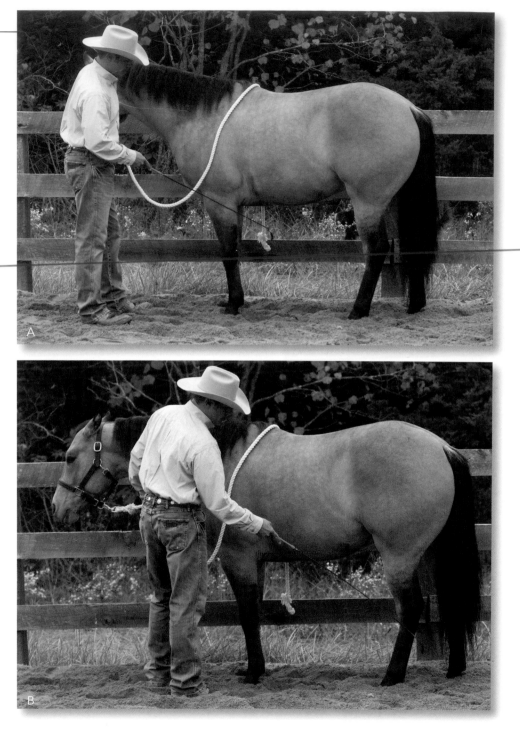

2   When the horse is relaxed about having his legs and feet touched, ask him to go forward, tracking left, stop him, and ask him to stand still. Then, apply pressure with the flat of your right hand to his shoulder above his forearm. When the horse moves or shifts away from that pressure, release the pressure. Repeat until the horse does it correctly five to seven times in a row: Apply pressure. Release the pressure when he moves away from it.

3   Soon, the horse will start cocking the foot beneath the shoulder receiving pressure (fig. 8.23). Once he has cocked it, reach down (use your left hand on the horse's left side; use your right hand on the horse's right side), grasp the horse's leg above the fetlock joint, and slowly pick it up.

4   Hold the horse's leg for no more than one or two seconds, and then put it back down.

8.23   *I apply pressure to Dillon's shoulder and remove it immediately when he shifts his weight off the corresponding foot.*

5   Repeat the process: Add pressure to the shoulder and ask the horse to shift his weight off that leg. Quickly reach down and pick up the leg. Hold it for a second, and drop it. Do this over and over.

6   Soon, the horse will associate the application of light pressure on his shoulder with picking up the respective leg. The horse will pick his foot off the ground a little bit. When that happens, start holding the leg a little bit longer—first, for two to three seconds. Then longer—for four to five seconds. Hold the leg longer and longer until the horse allows you to hold it for 30 to 60 seconds before putting it down.

Treating Trailer Trouble

If your horse won't load, you aren't alone. Many horse owners, at some point in their life, come in contact with a horse that doesn't like the trailer. When I started my career working with horses, I actually made a living *just* teaching horses to load on a trailer.

Teaching a horse to load is a long process, but it's very simple. Unlike some other behavior problems, *anybody* can do it. Of the thousands of horses I've taught to load, every single one not only went on the trailer during the initial training process, but also continued to load willingly long after.

BEFORE YOU BEGIN

1   Evaluate the horse's fear level when in the vicinity of the trailer. The horse should be unconcerned and unafraid. If the horse is uptight or reacting out of fear, don't increase his stress level by asking him to load. Instead, work with him on Basic Control (see p. 90) until he becomes calm and relaxed.

2   Determine what kind of refusal the horse is going to give you. Walk him toward the trailer and observe his reaction. At some point, his feet will

TRAILER MATTERS

When it comes to trailering, remember to stay safe. When evaluating your trailer for safety:

1   Make sure that the floor, walls, and dividers of the trailer are solid and safe.

2   Determine whether or not the horse has enough headroom. You don't want to put a 17.3-hand horse in a 6' 5" trailer, for instance.

3   Be certain that the horse has adequate space inside the trailer. The trailer must be wide enough and long enough for the horse to fit into comfortably without causing claustrophobia.

4   Be sure the trailer doesn't have any rust spots, nails, loose boards, or other hazards that could injure the horse. Also, check to ascertain that no bees, wasps, or hornets have taken up residence since the last time the trailer was used.

5   Make sure that the manger area is small enough that the horse can't jump up into it or snake his head around and interfere with another horse that may be trailered alongside him.

6   Check your tires and springs. Be sure they have good treads and are properly inflated.

7   Make sure your hitch is good. Also ascertain that your hitch is on correctly and that your safety chains are on. Note: Do not practice trailer loading without having the trailer hitched to the truck.

8   Make sure that the entrance to the trailer has a bumper in good condition to keep the horse from scraping his legs during entry or exit.

9   The trailer mats should be thick, sturdy, well-fitting, and durable.

10 Check that all door latches and "butt bars" are strong and close properly. (Any internal dividers should securely latch open and shut.)

11 Before you go anywhere: Double check the condition and connection of your emergency brake cable and your lights. Check running lights, brake lights, turn signals, and other signals.

9.3 A & B   *A safe trailer has solid floors, sturdy walls and doors, ample room, and is free of hazards that could harm the horse during transport (A). An unsafe trailer may have bad flooring, rust spots, and other rough edges, small claustrophobic spaces, inadequate ventilation, poor tires, or other problems (B). It only takes one hazard to make a trailer a danger to your horse.*

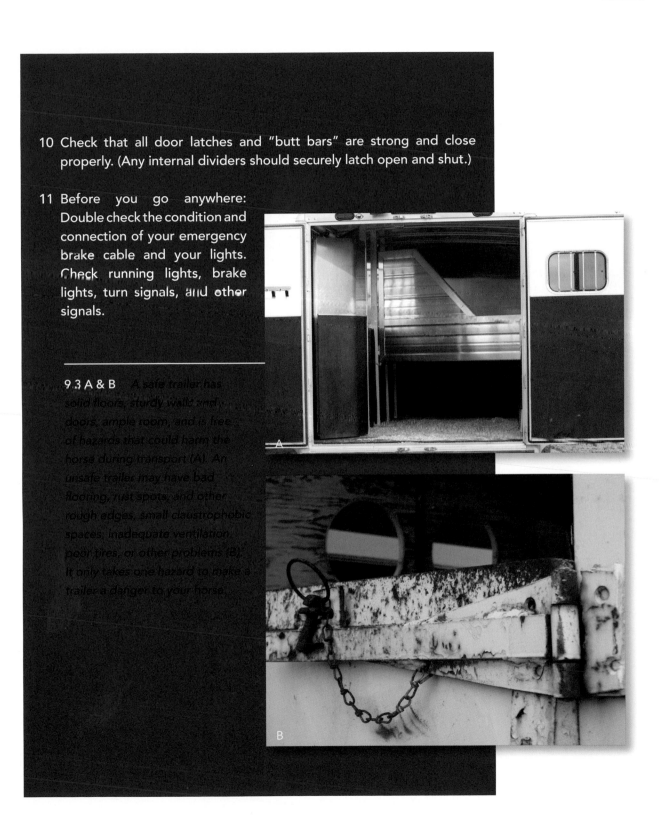

1   Begin in a safe area with a simple obstacle such as a ground pole along the fence line. Allow the horse to sniff the obstacle briefly. Walk backward as you did in teaching him Basic Control (see p. 90), and lead the horse back and forth over the obstacle until he navigates it calmly.

2   Then, walk the horse over the ground pole and back him up over it.

3   Repeat the exercise, this time walking (*not* jumping) over a cavalletti approximately 8 to 12 inches above the ground, placed perpendicular to the fence. Circle the horse around you, reverse direction, and switch sides so you are not pinned up against the fence. Then slowly navigate the cavalletti in the opposite direction.

4   Now lay out a tarp on the ground along the fence. The tarp should be at least 6 foot square, in good repair, and anchored securely with ground poles. (Note: *Do not* do this exercise with a horse wearing shoes. The nails of the shoes can act as cleats and affix the tarp to the horse, resulting in a wreck of epic proportions.) Ask the horse to walk calmly across the tarp and negotiate it from both directions (fig. 9.4).

9.4   *Walking the horse across a series of obstacles such as ground poles, cavalletti, and tarps teaches him to place his feet over and on top of increasingly foreign objects. Do not graduate to a more challenging obstacle until the horse will calmly accept the "easier" one.*

9.5   *I practice walking Dillon up onto a low raised platform, and backing him off. I incrementally have him place first one, then two, then three, then all four feet on the platform. I back him off after each incremental success.*

5   Along the fence line, set up a raised platform made of sturdy pallets with a new piece of ¾- or 1-inch plywood screwed securely on top. Allow the horse to briefly sniff the platform. Cue the horse to move forward and step on the platform. When the horse puts one foot on it, praise him and back him off it. Continue in stages: first one foot, then two, then three, then all four. Use taps on the girth line for the front feet and on the hip for the back feet. Back the horse straight off after every step (fig. 9.5).

6   When the horse is comfortable walking on and backing off the platform, encourage him to step on the platform and stand calmly while you pet him.

7   Construct a "mock trailer" around the platform that is open on only one end. (An easy and affordable version: PVC pipe held together with duct tape or several barrels lined up can be used to delineate the "trailer" area.) Allow the horse to sniff the construction. Ask the horse to walk onto the platform, stand quietly while you pet him, then back off when asked. Repeat this until he seems comfortable with the process (fig. 9.6).

9.6 *I walk Dillon into the framed-in "mock trailer." I'll pet him while he stands quietly, then back him off and walk him on repeatedly until he is completely content with the process.*

WHAT SHOULD I DO WHEN...?

PROBLEM:
My horse throws his shoulder into me when I ask him to back up over an obstacle.

SOLUTION:
If the horse tries to shove you out of his way, put your hand holding the lead rope against his shoulder and increase the pressure by pushing him backward.

9.7 *I let Dillon walk into the "mock trailer" and stand quietly while I remain by the "rear door."*

8   If your "mock trailer" is open-sided (if you use PVC pipes, for example) now use a tarp or sturdy cardboard to enclose the sides. Walk the horse on, ask him to stand quietly while you pet him, then back him off. After he walks on, stands, and backs off in a calm and relaxed manner, have him walk on to the raised platform while you remain by the "rear door" area (fig. 9.7). When you can do that five to seven times correctly, it's time to move on to the real thing.

Before asking a horse to go on the trailer, make sure everything is arranged to encourage his success:

➠   If using a slant load trailer, secure the dividers by locking them in place, and load the horse on and off the *rear* section of the trailer (furthest from the hitch).

➠   Make sure the door hinges are out of the way so neither you nor the horse will get injured.

➠   Inspect the trailer for safety (see Trailer Matters, p. 124).

➠   Evaluate the surroundings for distractions and safety hazards.

Slowly, patiently, introduce the horse to the trailer in a step-by-step, methodical manner:

1   Move the horse up to the very edge of the Yellow Zone by taking him to the place near the trailer where he starts to become resistant (see p. 122).

2   Tap the horse at the girth line and ask him to take a single step forward (see p. 81). When he does, back him up and return him to his Green Zone. Repeat this process, gradually coming closer and closer to the trailer.

3   Allow the horse to sniff the trailer and inspect it, if he wishes (fig. 9.8).

4   Back the horse quietly away from the trailer, then lead him up to it again. Ask him to put one foot on the ramp or step, then back him off. Repeat this over and over. (Note: Repeatedly backing the horse off serves to prepare him for the unloading process.)

WHAT SHOULD I DO WHEN...?

PROBLEM:
My horse swings his hips off to the side instead of walking straight over the obstacle.

SOLUTION:
Use your dressage whip to tap the horse on the hip that swings out and keep him straight. Tap him near the flank until the corresponding leg moves underneath his belly. When that happens, stop tapping for a moment. Then resume tapping, and releasing, until the hips are back in line with his shoulders.

9.8 *When the horse approaches the trailer, do not be in a hurry to make him get on. I briefly allow Dillon to examine the setup, sniff it, and familiarize himself with it.*

WHAT SHOULD I DO WHEN...?

PROBLEM:
My horse speeds up when walking over an obstacle.

SOLUTION:
Watch the horse's body language. If he tries to run over you or jump over the obstacle, stop his feet by putting your lead rope hand up high near his head, and back him up over the obstacle immediately (see p. 102 for more on this technique).

5   Go through the same process to ask the horse to put both his front feet on the trailer ramp or step. When he does so, pat him, rub him all over, reassure him, and encourage him to stay there for a bit. Back him off the trailer, walk the two front feet back on, and reassure him again (fig. 9.9).

6   When the horse is comfortable placing his two front feet on the trailer and backing off again, ask him to walk his entire body onto the trailer. (Note: If your trailer has a ramp, you may have to take a few extra steps to accustom the horse first to this surface, and then to the actual trailer entrance.) You may need to use the cue you taught him earlier for stepping forward with a hind leg: the tap on the hip (see Before You Begin, p. 121). Once he is on, allow him to stand quietly *without* tying him, placing the butt bar in position, or closing the door (fig. 9.10). You do not want him to feel trapped. Back him off, walk him away from the trailer, return, and load him again. (If you've done your homework properly, backing the horse off shouldn't present a problem.)

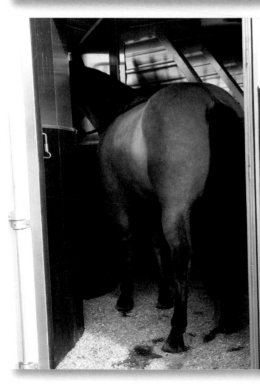

9.9 *Let the horse get used to standing with his front feet in the trailer. I rub Dillon all over and reward him for going this far in.*

9.10 *Load the horse all the way onto the trailer, but do not tie him or enclose him at first. Let him get used to standing quietly inside, then back him off and load him on repeatedly before you take the next step and "lock" him in.*

*WHAT SHOULD
I DO WHEN...?*

PROBLEM:
My horse bolts backward out
of the trailer.

SOLUTION:
When the horse runs
backward out of the trailer, go
with him—don't try to stop
him. Follow him backward
until he stops. When he does,
that place becomes the new
boundary of the Yellow Zone.
Begin again, asking the horse
to gradually move forward
and calmly back up on
command as before.

STEPS FOR SAFELY SECURING THE HORSE IN THE TRAILER

1   Do not close the trailer doors or tie the horse in a trailer until the horse loads calmly and stands comfortably inside *without* being tied or otherwise contained.

2   Enlist an assistant to unlatch the trailer door from the trailer side and swing it partially closed. When the door is three-quarters shut, affix the "butt bar" securely in place.

3   Close the door and lock it.

4   Finally, tie the horse securely.

7   Load the horse successfully at least five to seven times. Continue until the horse stands comfortably in the trailer without anyone in there with him, without being tied, and without the doors being closed. Only when the horse is happy to stand quietly inside and does not try to escape should you close the doors and secure him (see sidebar, above).

8   Practice loading and unloading the horse in the trailer. Close the doors and secure him inside. Do this hundreds and hundreds of times. Continue working on the issue until the horse is *completely comfortable* being in the trailer.e

PRACTICE PATIENCE

Training a horse to load on a trailer is all about *patience*. It is not a process that should be rushed. It also should *not* involve any of the following actions (or those like them):

→ Threading the horse's lead rope through the trailer window and using leverage to pull the horse onto the trailer.

→ Clasping hands with someone else, linking your arms behind the horse, and pushing him in the trailer.

→ Using a lunge line around the horse's hindquarters to "squash" him into the trailer.

→ Standing behind the horse and whipping him or otherwise trying to scare him on to the trailer.

Revisit Your Groundwork

Remember, when it comes to working with horses, everything is interconnected. What happens on the ground affects what happens in the saddle. If your horse is behaving badly under saddle, the first thing you should do is revisit his groundwork and reinforce good ground manners. When the horse behaves well on the ground, his behavior under saddle will improve dramatically.

Before you begin working to correct under saddle problems, be sure to review the in-hand exercises for Basic Control (see p. 90). In my experience, most behavioral issues under saddle stem from one of three things:

The horse has a poor "Go" cue.

The horse has a poor "Stop" cue.

The horse has not been adequately exposed to a variety of obstacles and experiences.

Most behavioral issues that show up when a horse is being ridden will dramatically decrease or be eliminated entirely if the trainer focuses on in-hand exercises that target the root of the problem. The final step, then, is taking the actions performed for the trainer on the ground and connecting them with similar actions executed under saddle.

In the pages that follow, I have identified the behavioral problems I most commonly encounter under saddle. For each one, I assume that the handler has already spent considerable time working on the Basic Controls in-hand and itemize a systematic way to eliminate the unwanted behavior that builds upon what the horse already knows.

TRAINING TOOLS

Train using the tack in which you normally ride. The following readily available tools are the only things I use to fix most common behavioral issues that arise under saddle:

➣ A round pen or a safe arena that doesn't have any wire. You need a contained area with a *solid fence*. Note: As I've mentioned, I am not against using a round pen as a safe enclosure for horse training—only the popular "round penning" methods so often seen today (see my arguments on p. 29).

➣ A well-balanced saddle that fits both you and the horse.

➣ A full-cheek snaffle bit.

➣ A balanced bridle.

➣ 10- or 12-foot continuous rope reins.

10.1   *Well-chosen tack and a safe working environment are the only tools you should need to re-train your horse.*

Bolting

10.2 *Bolting away from something that frightens him is one of the horse's most basic survival instincts. When a sound, object, or animal triggers the fear response, the horse will naturally run from it.*

Horses bolt for a variety of reasons. One of the most common is fear. As I discussed earlier in the book, horses are born with fear. They embody it. They *are* fear (fig. 10.2). If your horse bolts once out of fear, chances are high that he will do it again.

Bolting is a very dangerous behavior, but one that you can rehabilitate. In order to stop a horse from bolting, you need to develop a means of communicating with him so that you can layer desired responses over the undesired behavior and eventually make it a thing of the past (fig. 10.3).

If your horse bolts, ask yourself, "What is my horse *not* doing that I wish he *would* do?" The answer, of course, is: he's not standing quietly and ignoring the outside influence that caused him to bolt in the first place. Work to identify what is triggering the fear response. "Triggers" can include:

➨ The rider getting into the saddle.

➨ Other horses.

10.3   *Exposing the horse to a wide variety of experiences and systematically layering desired responses over the horse's instinctive behavior will enable the horse to replace his automatic flight response with a more measured, calmer approach to outside stimuli. Here, Dillon stands calmly near the bright-colored umbrella.*

10.4   *Expose the horse to a variety of distracting items that gradually increase in intensity, such as I am here with ground poles, a tarp, and the umbrella. Remember: the goal is to never force the horse out of his Green Zone, but to slowly raise the bar on his fear response without triggering it.*

- ❥   Going through gates or other "enclosed" areas.

- ❥   Foreign objects along the trail.

Then, target your training to systematically introduce your horse to those triggers in a controlled setting. The goal is to acclimatize the horse to these triggers so gradually that he will remain in the Green Zone and never feel compelled to react with a fear response.

IN-HAND BOLT-BUSTING EXERCISES

1   Review the Basic Controls (p. 90). I also recommend using the Connection Clock with bolters, so if you haven't yet familiarized yourself with it, have a look at my *Connection* DVD (see p. 75 for details).

2   Work the horse over and around a variety of distractions and obstacles, including ground poles, cavalletti, tarps, mounting blocks, saddle pads, noisemakers, and others. Thoroughly accustom the horse to the sight, feel, sound, and movement of each distraction (fig. 10.4).

EMERGENCY STOPS

If you are riding a horse with a bolting issue, you must have a way of stopping him in case of an emergency.

Some people will tell you that the way to stop a bolter, or to stop a horse that is going too fast, is to disengage his hindquarters. *I strongly discourage this.* If you disengage a horse's hindquarters, there is a high likelihood that the horse could be thrown off balance. In extreme cases, the horse could even trip or take a tumble with you on him. Another reason I discourage this practice is because disengaging the horse's hindquarters really doesn't *stop* the horse. It merely turns him to the left or to the right.

If the horse bolts while you are in the saddle, the key is to get off the horse, get out of the saddle, and do more ground work until the horse no longer bolts as a fear response. In my opinion, the best way to stop a bolter is to apply what many people call a "pulley rein" or a "cavalry stop." Pick up one rein, raising the hand holding it up high, above the horse's ears. At the same time move the other hand, on the other rein, back toward your hips. Do this quickly, firmly, and decisively. When the pulley rein has been applied, the horse's head comes up, and his stride becomes short and choppy. His stride will shorten to the point where he stops. When that happens, dismount *immediately*.

10.5 *To apply the "pulley rein" or "cavalry stop," pick up one rein and raise it high above the horse's ears. Pull at the same time, pulling the other rein back toward your hips. Do this quickly, firmly, and decisively. When you apply pressure to both reins quickly and firmly, Dillon's head comes up, and his stride dramatically shortens.*

When riding a horse that has bolted, do not attempt to jump off or launch yourself toward the ground. The likelihood of you getting hurt is very high. First, stop the horse. Wait until all four feet stop moving—if only for an instant—and *then* dismount. Use common sense and stay safe by raising the near side rein: pull it up hard and tight to keep the horse's head turned in the direction of where you are dismounting.

As soon as your feet hit the ground, start working the horse using the in-hand exercises in chapter 8 (see p. 89). They are the key to a good ride in the saddle.

BOLT-BUSTING UNDER SADDLE IN AN ARENA

Be sure to set your horse (and yourself) up for success. If your horse has a bolting issue, the last thing you want to do is ride him in a 20-acre pasture, or an even larger open space! Work him for a while in a contained environment, such as a round pen or medium-sized arena, until you have worked through the worst of his bolting problem.

If at any time the horse begins moving forward faster than you want him to, back him up. First, stop him with a "pulley rein" or "cavalry stop" (see p. 139). Shut down the horse's forward motion. Then back the horse up, followed by moving him forward again. Repeat this, going forward and then backing up until the horse moves forward calmly and backs up willingly, without "rooting" his face forward or leaning into the bit.

The following exercises are important because they occupy the horse's mind, keep him busy, and give him something other than his fear to think about. They get him used to working quietly under saddle without spooking or giving in to the fear response.

1.   While the horse is standing quietly, pick up on the right rein. Add pressure to it until the horse moves the corresponding front foot (the right) back (fig. 10.6). Then immediately release the rein pressure and reward the horse. Repeat on the left side: Pick up on the left rein. Add pressure to it until the horse moves the corresponding front foot (the left) back. Immediately release the rein pressure and reward the horse.

10.6   *Pressure on one rein causes the corresponding foreleg to move backward. As soon as Dillon responds correctly on one side, I release the rein pressure on that side and apply it to the other side to influence the other foreleg.*

2   Move the horse forward. Let him take three to five steps. Then stop him (see Stop on p. 83). Again apply pressure alternately to the reins: inside (meaning closer to the center of the arena), outside, inside, outside... and back the horse up. Go up and down the rail, moving forward several steps, stopping, and backing up repeatedly.

3   Now circle. Use the inside rein to apply slight pressure every time the horse's inside leg goes forward. Apply pressure and release in rhythm with the horse, shortening the horse's stride on that side and causing him to turn in a circle. If, at any time, the horse bolts forward, apply firm pressure with the *outside rein*. Then alternate both reins as before—inside, outside, inside, outside—and back the horse up before asking him to move forward again.

4   When the horse circles correctly in both directions, practice serpentines. Create a half-circle to the right, then to the left, then to the right, and so on. The purpose of serpentines is to gain better control of the horse's feet and get his brain engaged.

5   Set up two cones, barrels, or buckets about 20 feet apart and work the horse in figure eights around them (figs. 10.7 A & B). Begin at a walk, progress to a trot, then canter when the horse is nice and relaxed. (If at any time, the horse bolts and takes off with you, immediately raise one hand high, pull the other to your hip, and back him up.)

6   Continue making the arena exercises progressively more difficult. Set up additional cones, buckets, or barrels. Ride in serpentines, figure eights, and circles around them, in both directions, at different speeds. Keep the horse's brain engaged and his feet moving. Remove the choice of when to speed up and when to slow down from him. If he starts to bolt, either stop him and back him up, as before, or simply turn him to the left or to the right, make a transition to a slower gait, and continue working on the current exercise.

BOLT-BUSTING UNDER SADDLE ON THE TRAIL

The trail is an uncontrolled, uncontained area. Work the horse in the open *only* after you have successfully completed all of your in-hand work and all your arena work, and are confident that you have a solid emergency stop, should the need arise (see p. 139).

**WHAT SHOULD
I DO WHEN...?**

PROBLEM:
My horse tries to bolt even while I'm working him in-hand, reviewing the Basic Controls.

SOLUTION:
When working your horse in hand, you should always make sure that you are in a safe, contained environment. If your horse decides to bolt, don't be a hero. There is no point in holding onto the horse and risking getting dragged around the arena and badly injured. Let the horse go. Then catch him, regroup, and begin working him again. Take extra care not to push the horse into triggering his flight response. Progress with your training very slowly and methodically. And remember to reward the horse for exhibiting the behavior you desire.

10.7 A & B   *I work Dillon in a figure eight around two markers approximately 20 feet apart, bending him both right and left, and progressing from the walk, to the trot, to the canter as he is ready. This simple exercise keeps Dillon's brain engaged and gives him something constructive to do.*

1   Before you go anywhere on the trail, review your basic controls, stop and start the horse, back him up, and walk, trot, and canter him on a small- to medium-sized circle. Make sure he's willing to listen to you in a moderately controlled environment before you venture out.

2   When you do hit the trail, keep the horse's brain engaged. Practice transitions and turning. Go from a walk to a trot, then back to a walk. Steer the horse right and left, do some serpentines and circles. When you are comfortable at a walk and a trot, practice transitions from a canter to a trot in circles (fig. 10.8).

When riding a horse with a history of bolting on the trail, even after you have done your in-hand training and arena work, always take along a friend or two to ride with you and provide assistance if necessary. Follow the same steps as outlined in Separation Anxiety (see p. 153), and give your horse something to engage his mind and keep him focused on you.

I don't care what anyone says, there is no possible way that you can desensitize a horse to everything that he might ever encounter in his entire life. It's just impossible. However, you *can* ask a horse to respond correctly and listen to you whenever you begin to notice him approaching the Yellow Zone (see p. 39). The key to stopping a horse from spooking and bolting when something frightens him is training: Train the horse to listen to his rider rather than simply give in to his fear.

10.8 *When on the trail, I keep Dillon's attention with little "jobs" and exercises. I ride in circles and serpentines. I practice transitions from one gait to another. This keeps Dillon thinking more about me than about his surroundings.*

WHAT SHOULD I DO WHEN...?

PROBLEM:
I don't understand how working my horse in-hand or in a contained arena on basic patterns and exercises will teach him not to bolt when I'm on the trail.

SOLUTION:
Arena exercises teach the horse to use his mind, to think first and react later. They also teach him to listen to his rider (you) for direction. They get him used to listening to you and to responding to your cues. Done correctly, simple arena exercises, both in-hand and under saddle, are the key to a safe, bolt-free horse.

Bucking

Bucking is a Red Zone activity. It is not something you ever want to encourage the horse to do. So, it is important to make sure that when you ride, you take steps not to allow the horse to express *any* type of bucking behavior (fig. 10.9).

Eliminating the buck from a horse's repertoire of bad behaviors is done through the process of *deletion* (for more on this topic, see p. 34). Deletion is a systematic way of telling the horse that a buck, or anything like it, is the *wrong response*. The way to delete bucking is to simply stop the bad behavior as it is being expressed and repeat only behavior that is desired.

10.9   *Bucking is always a Red Zone action. No bucking is to ever be tolerated or excused. If left unchecked and uncorrected, bucking will only escalate into what could rapidly become a very dangerous situation.*

THE FEAR FACTOR

Years ago, I encountered a horse who bucked me off. The physical injuries were bad enough. But the emotional impact stayed behind and took some time for me to work through.

If you have been bucked off once, you really don't want it to happen again. When I meet a person with a horse that bucks, the main thing that person wants to address is his or her fear. That fear of losing control, hitting the ground, and getting injured can be crippling, even for good riders and experienced trainers.

If you find that the fear of getting bucked off is interfering with your ability to ride and train your horse, recognize the problem. Don't risk getting seriously injured. Don't allow misplaced pride to endanger you. Take your horse to a reputable professional who will apply sound principles of horsemanship to fix the problem.

WHY DOES MY HORSE BUCK?

Bucking begins as an incorrect response to a "go forward" cue. The horse is confused over the request and he displays a fear response, which in this case is bucking. So what do many people do? They try to ride it out. *Yeehaw*! And what does that promote? Riding the bucking horse allows the horse to practice bucking! Each time the horse bucks, he's perfecting the unwanted, dangerous behavior.

It is never prudent to allow the horse to buck. Don't let anyone tell you that it's okay "while he's getting warmed up" or because "he's feeling good." Some well-meaning but ill-informed people advise allowing the horse to "buck himself out." This not only hinders the training process, but it also strengthens the bucking response. Bucking is *never* acceptable behavior. If you allow the horse to continue bucking under saddle, ultimately someone will get hurt. Instead of encouraging bucking, delete such negative behavior and allow those responses you *want* to become more consolidated.

A horse bucks for many reasons. Some of these might include physical issues, as pain can cause a horse to erupt in a bucking fit. Enlist a veterinarian's help to determine whether an underlying physical problem could be causing the horse's bucking. Have the vet check the horse thoroughly, including his back, feet, legs, and teeth.

Consider the nutritional aspects that contribute to your horse's behavior. Take care to feed a balanced ration that contains all the necessary nutrients for the horse. Make sure you are not feeding the horse too much sugar, starch, or carbohydrates, or giving him feed that overloads his system with more energy than he needs. Your hay, too, needs evaluating. Feed a top quality hay that imparts good, dependable nutrition.

If you have systematically eliminated physical and nutritional problems as a source of the horse's bucking, observe the horse in his surroundings. Analyze the details as objectively as possible:

➡ How big is his stall? Does he have enough room to move around in it?

➡ How long is he stalled per day?

➡ Does the horse exhibit any type of aberrant behavior when he is contained? Does he weave, crib, or paw in his stall? If so, how long after he has been contained does he begin such actions?

➡ Consider the horse's pasture and downtime environment. Does he have a large pasture where he can get out and exercise?

Remember, a horse needs a lot of pasture time. At least 10 to 12 hours a day is ideal. Horses that are stalled extensively and that receive very little pasture time are prone to a whole list of bad behaviors, including (but not limited to) bucking (fig. 10.10).

After you have taken the horse's physical condition and environment into consideration, closely inspect the tack you use, both on and off the horse. Poor saddle fit is a common cause of bucking problems.

➡ If the saddle is *too long* for the horse, it will ride up on the horse's shoulders in front and interfere with the horse's loins and hips in the back.

➡ If the saddle is *too wide* for the horse, it will put direct pressure on the horse's withers and spine.

➡ If the saddle is *too narrow* for the horse, it will pinch his withers, interfere with the movement of the shoulder blades, and constrict his spine.

10.10 *Horses require activity and unrestricted freedom to move around. A routine that includes extensive stall time and minimal turnout virtually invites a horse to develop unwanted behaviors, including bucking.*

➧   If the saddle has an *asymmetrical* or *damaged tree*, it will pinch and interfere with the horse, causing irritation and possible physical damage, regardless of how well-trained the horse may be.

➧   Excessively loose or overly tight girthing can be another cause of bucking problems, even on a well-fitting saddle.

Finally, consider the level of your horse's training. If he has only been ridden a few times and has bucked once or twice, that's a very different problem to solve than an older horse that has made it a habit to buck in order to unload his rider.

PRE-RIDE EVALUATION

As I mentioned, the horse that bucks has an issue with going forward. Revisit the horse's "Go" and "Stop" cues (see pp. 81 and 83). Make note of how responsive the horse is to your cues.

➧   Check how willingly the horse allows himself to be touched all over. Of special concern are areas where the horse flinches when gently touched.

➧   Evaluate your horse's willingness to be saddled. Saddle him in phases, using a customized version of the Station Game (see p. 99):

1   Gently flap the saddle pad around the horse, and rub it all over his body and his legs (fig. 10.11). Pay attention to any adverse reaction the horse may exhibit.

2   Place the saddle on the horse's back.

3   Rock the saddle back and forth a bit.

4   Flap the girth and the stirrups gently.

5   Slap the saddle gently.

Note how the horse handles the saddling experience. The purpose of this is to determine whether the horse's bucking stems from issues he may have with the saddle or the saddling process. Any negative reactions on the horse's part will indicate where you need to start with your training.

WHAT SHOULD I DO WHEN...?

PROBLEM:
When I ride, I can feel my horse bunch up underneath me and act like he's going to buck. This scares me.

SOLUTION:
When you feel your horse "think" about bucking, *get off*. When you feel the horse's back start to round and arch, when his head goes straight down or pops up in the air, and when his stride gets short and choppy, *dismount*! Go back to your groundwork and review the things the horse needs to know. This is a long-term process. Rehabilitating a bucking horse doesn't happen in a day or a week. There is no quick fix. Do not endanger yourself by trying to ride the horse through the buck.

If you can tack up your horse while he stands quietly, with no fear behaviors triggering a negative reaction to the process, then prepare to mount up and continue the evaluation from the saddle. Before you get on, however, review how the horse reacted the last few times he was ridden. Ask questions including:

◆   What caused the horse to enter the Yellow Zone?

◆   What set him off and resulted in bucking?

◆   How long had he been ridden before he bucked?

◆   How responsive was he to going forward, turning left and right, and stopping?

◆   How long did he buck when he started?

Make note of the answers. They will help you realize where to start your retraining and enable you to form a plan of action.

10.11   *Evaluate the horse's response to every phase of the saddling process. If the horse has an aversion to something as simple and basic as a flapping saddle pad, it could be disastrous to progress with saddling and riding him instead of taking the time to delete the adverse reaction.*

STAYING SAFE WITH A BUCKER

If your horse has a bucking problem, the last place you should be is in the saddle. The instant any bucking issues arise, review your groundwork and solidify the horse's responsiveness to you in-hand before you trust your life to the horse and get on him.

In the event of the horse erupting in a bucking fit while you are mounted, *do not try to ride it out*. Staying on will only teach the horse to buck better and harder. Stop the horse as quickly as possible (use the "pulley rein" or "cavalry stop" described on p. 139), dismount, and do more of the in hand groundwork that will correct the problem.

Don't take chances! Your safety is always the most important aspect of horse training.

MOUNTING THE BUCKER

Mount the horse in stages. Go about the process incrementally, making careful note of the horse's reaction. If the horse stands quietly, proceed to the next step. If the horse's head shoots up in the air, if he flinches, or if he exhibits any other kind of Yellow Zone behavior, *do not continue*. Instead, make note of the reaction. This will tell you where you need to focus your systematic desensitizing and training efforts:

1   Put pressure on the stirrup.

2   Practice putting your foot in and out of the stirrup.

3   Place your foot in the stirrup and bounce up and down a few times.

4   Hop up on the saddle, balance with one foot in the stirrup, pet the horse on the other side, or flap the opposite stirrup (fig. 10.12).

5   Mount and dismount several times before asking the horse to move forward with you on board.

WHAT SHOULD I DO WHEN...?

PROBLEM:
My horse isn't bucking anymore, but he still kicks out with his hind legs occasionally.

SOLUTION:
Treat kicking out as if it were a buck. Address it the same way. Stop the horse's feet. Shut down his forward motion. Back him up. Then immediately put him back into the same gait he was in before he kicked out. Do this consistently every time the horse kicks out. Remember: *Every* time the horse gives you the wrong response, *delete* the response and repeat the cue for the desired behavior.

10.12   *Do not be in a hurry to mount the horse and commit your safety to him. Stand balanced on one side of the saddle and make sure the horse will readily accept seeing you on the other side of his body. Here I lean over Dillon's back and pet him on the opposite side before swinging all the way up into the saddle.*

THE RULES OF SAFE MOUNTING

Before you begin to mount any horse—especially one that has a history of bucking—make sure you are not wearing any loose clothing. Tuck your shirt into your jeans, and remove all jewelry. Don't have anything on your body that could possibly get hung up or stuck on the saddle.

When you do mount, keep your center of gravity as low as possible (fig. 10.13 A). Don't stand in the stirrup with your head and shoulders high (fig. 10.13 B). If the horse were to move suddenly, you would overbalance and fall to the ground like a lawn dart. Stay low to the saddle and to the horse.

Anytime you work with a horse that you are unsure of, have a handler hold the horse while you mount.

10.13 A & B   *When mounting, keep a low center of gravity and maintain a low profile to avoid the likelihood of overbalancing should the horse suddenly move (A). When I mount incorrectly (B), my head and shoulders are held too high. If Dillon were to move quickly, I would almost certainly fall.*

**WHAT SHOULD
I DO WHEN...?**

PROBLEM:

My horse bucked a little, but it was so minor it wasn't that hard to ride out, and he only did it once. I'd rather stay on and deal with it than dismount every time. Besides, I don't want to teach him that a tiny buck is a way to get me off his back.

SOLUTION:

If the horse bucks in such a manner that it merely annoys you, rather than threatens your life, you can remain in the saddle, but by all means *correct the behavior*. Do a downward transition to the stop and immediately back up. Do this faithfully each time the horse begins to buck, and you'll *delete* the behavior (see p. 34). Then give the "Go" cue immediately, and you'll recondition the horse to the correct response. This is the basis of good horse training: *Allow* the horse to practice the *correct behavior* and *don't allow* him to express the *wrong behavior*.

BUCK-BUSTING UNDER SADDLE IN AN ARENA

We've discussed how bucking is always the result of a "go forward" issue. Therefore, when working to rehabilitate a bucking horse, the focus is on perfecting the "go forward" cue.

1   In a large round pen, medium-sized arena, or other safe, contained space, mount the horse. Ask him to walk forward. Walk along the rail, or in a circle. Stop the horse in three steps (see Stop, p. 83). Walk him forward again.

2   As with the habitual bolter, practice arena exercises such as circles, figure eights, serpentines, changes of direction, and transitions. Keep the horse's mind busy. Give him something to do *other* than buck.

3   I advise using the Connection Clock under saddle to get control of the horse's shoulders. I explain the Clock in detail on my DVD *Connection*, but for the purposes of buck-busting, here is a simple way to connect the inside rein (meaning closer to the inside of the arena) to the inside foreleg, and the outside rein to the outside foreleg (before you begin, refamiliarize yourself with the brief description and illustration of the Connection Clock on p. 75): Move the horse forward. Apply slight pressure straight back toward your belt with the outside rein (the left rein if tracking to the right) and apply leading rein pressure with the inside rein (the right rein if tracking to the right). This slight leading pressure on the inside rein moves the horse's shoulders laterally onto a different path than his hips so he executes either a shoulder-fore or shoulder-in, depending on the degree of lateral movement. Use your outside leg to encourage the horse to move away from the outside of the circle toward what would be "one o'clock"—shoulder-fore—on the Connection Clock (fig. 10.14). Then try toward "two o'clock" (shoulder-in), switch directions, and move the horse toward "eleven" and "ten o'clock."

4   Place several cones or buckets in a straight line along the center line of the arena. Practice serpentines and circles around the cones to gain control of the horse's feet. Encourage the horse to keep his head relaxed and down. Start at the walk. Move to the trot. Then practice transitions between the two gaits.

10.14 *Controlling the horse's shoulders encourages him to concentrate more on you than on bucking and misbehaving. I apply slight backward rein pressure with the outside (left) rein and slight leading pressure on the inside (right) rein to move Dillon's shoulders laterally onto a different path than his hips, executing a mild shoulder-fore. I like to think of slight pressure to the right as guiding the horse's shoulders toward "one o'clock" (see the Connection Clock, p. 75) while slight pressure to the left takes them toward "eleven o'clock." Increased rein pressure increases the lateral bend to that of a shoulder-in, moving the horse more toward "two" or "ten o'clock," respectively.*

5   When you are ready, add the canter to your gaits. Work in straight lines at first. Lope two or three strides, then trot immediately. Lope a bit more, then trot again. Stay light on the horse's mouth, but shut him down before he gets too strong and thinks about bucking.

Separation Anxiety

If a horse is barn sour or buddy sour, he can evidence his separation anxiety in a variety of ways. Generally, however, he will become progressively less responsive to the rider, and increasingly more determined to either go "home" or stay with his friends.

ELIMINATING SEPARATION ANXIETY

Enlist the help of several friends to school their horses alongside yours. It is essential that the riders of the other horses understand the training process you will be using in order to eliminate separation anxiety. The bonus is, these exercises will negate the habit in their horses, as well.

As always, your goal is to keep your horse in the Green Zone (see p. 39). You want him to remain responsive to you and listening to your cues as you progress through this series of exercises designed to encourage him to focus on you more than on anything else.

1   Ride in a circle at the walk. Ask your fellow riders to position their horses head to tail, with one horse behind another. After one or two circles, have the rider at the rear "peel away" and ride a smaller, tighter circle, so he ends up at the front of the line (figs. 10.15 A–C). Practice this until all horses are comfortable at all places in the lineup: beginning, middle, or end.

2   Take turns having one rider stop his horse and stand still while the other riders circle him at a trot, or have several in the group stand in the middle while one horse circles at the trot (fig. 10.16).

3   Have all riders practice trotting in a circle. The instant any one horse breaks gait or bolts forward, all riders should immediately stop their horses and back up. Then resume trotting.

4   Practice riding together in a circle, then splitting up to ride in different parts of the arena for awhile, then coming together again. Repeat this over and over. Gradually do your individual workouts further and further apart from each other, putting greater distance between each horse.

10.15 A–C   *I enlist several friends and their horses, and we circle in single file at the walk, with enough space between our horses for safety (A). Since I am at the rear of the line, I begin to ride a smaller, tighter circle than the leaders (B), and rejoin the track of the original circle, now at the front of the line (C). We will continue this simple exercises until all the horses are comfortable at any position in the group.*

10.16 *The two other riders ask their horses to stand still and relaxed as Dillon and I trot around them in a large circle.*

5   Take your group out on the trail, and have one rider stop and either stand still or back up while the rest of you ride by. Remember, when riding a horse on the trail, the horse should be more responsive to you (the rider) than to anything or anyone else (fig. 10.17).

6   While out on the trail, put some distance between each horse, then have the lead horse stop, turn around, and ride toward you as the group continues forward. Pass each other, allowing enough distance between horses for safety, and continue riding in opposite directions without breaking gait or stride.

10.17 *When riding outside the arena, don't just "turn your brain off" and let your horse wander the trail on autopilot. Have a plan in mind. Keep him thinking. Stop him and start him. Steer him left and right. Speed up and slow down. Go forward and back up. Challenge him. Make what you are doing far more interesting than what his buddies are doing. Get his attention and keep it.*

The Last Word on Behavior Problems

By now, you have probably noticed that the method I use to reclaim problem horses and eradicate all behavior issues simply involves two steps:

1   First, analyze the situation. Identify what the horse is doing incorrectly and articulate what breakdown in communication is occurring.

2   Then, take incremental steps to accustom the horse to gradually exhibit more and more of the desired behavior, until that behavior becomes his new "normal" response.

The integration of modern psychology and traditional horsemanship has the potential to bridge the language barrier between horse and man. It allows us to further communicate with the horse in an understandable manner, and breaks down those walls that keep us from truly connecting with each other.

Using *deletion* to convey to the horse that he has made an incorrect response will help to clarify this language, and improve the horse-human relationship. It will develop more consistent, long-lasting partnerships and has the potential to cause far less conflict between horse and rider. The next time your horse is giving you the wrong response, simply delete that response and try again.

Remember, if you are clear, consistent, and concise, you can develop a language that will enable you to communicate with your horse in such a way that eliminates confusion and only improves your relationship.

10.18　*Developing clear, consistent, concise cues enables you to communicate with your horse and know that he absolutely understands you. This provides the foundation for a lifelong partnership of connecting those cues into a mutually understandable language that you both master together.*

Television

See more of Ryan Gingerich on his weekly show, "Ryan Gingerich: The Behaviorist," on RFD-TV. RFD-TV is a rural TV network available in 35 million homes around the globe. Find it on Dish channel 231 and DirecTV channel 345, as well as over 125 cable systems. Consult your local TV guide or visit www.ryangingerich.com for showtimes in your area.

Web Site

For up-to-date information, including clinic dates and live appearances, go to www.ryangingerich.com. There, you can join the Connection Club, and personally contact Ryan and other club members.

DVDs

Ryan leads you through the steps necessary to train the horse you've always wanted in his collection of educational DVDs. Features an ever-expanding series of titles, including the *5 Elements of Connective Horsemanship* series. Available from www.ryangingerich.com.

Recommended Books

Grandin, Temple, Ph.D. and Catherine Johnson. *Animals in Translation: Using the Mysteries of Autism to Decode Animal Behavior.* Harvest Books, 2006. Offers especially interesting and relevant observations about the emotional capacity of animals.

McLean, Andrew, Ph.D. *The Truth About Horses: A Guide to Understanding and Training Your Horse.* David & Charles, 2003. Words of wisdom and great insight from a brilliant behaviorist.

O'Connell, Robert L. *Ride of the Second Horseman.* Oxford University Press, 1999. Details Dr. David Anthony's archaeological excavation and findings at Dereivka, in the Ukraine, where he and his research team concluded that the Sredni Stog culture used domesticated horses for transportation as well as food at least 6,000 years ago.

Acknowledgments

This book is a culmination of the efforts of many. Without the support of those around me, I could never have completed such a concise representation of my methods. For those I have learned from, those who have supported me, and those who have inspired me—thank you.

Special thanks to all those who had a hand in making this project possible:

Gary Jordan for believing in me and pushing me toward my present path.

Dana Manar for her dedication to this project.

Kate Riordan for her sharp eye and editorial experience.

Tim Wolfe for always challenging me to explain myself more clearly.

Dr. Andrew McLean for his incredible insight into the horse's mind, for sharing his knowledge, and for challenging me to look past what I thought I knew.

Mr. Richard Shrake for being a mentor.

Mr. John Lyons for inspiring me to be a better trainer.

My parents for always believing in me and supporting my endeavors.

My wife for her love, support, and encouragement all these years

My children for keeping me honest and loving me unconditionally

Mostly, I would like to thank all the horses that have made me the trainer that I am. Without them, I would be nowhere.